"I have just finished reading Ken
it's really terrific. Ken is a good exam
who has prioritized his life with a proper perspective.
His ideas about fatherhood and role modeling as affected
by his Christianity are inspiring.
We can all gain wisdom from *The Home Field Advantage.*"

—MIKE HOLMGREN
HEAD COACH
GREEN BAY PACKERS

"Winning with my kids
is even more important than winning on the field.
Ken Ruettgers feels the same way— and it shows.
His book is filled with effective strategies and plays from over fifty fellow
pro athletes who have accepted the challenge to be role model
dads and are leading their kids to victory.
I believe men all across the country will be helped and inspired
by Ken's call for them to recognize and seize upon the very real
Home Field Advantage that is theirs for the taking."

REGGIE WHITE
ALL PRO DEFENSIVE END
GREEN BAY PACKERS

Ken Ruettgers is a big man...with an even bigger heart.
At 6'6" and 290 pounds he's prowled the trenches for twelve years
as an outstanding NFL tackle.
But there's one small boy and two even smaller girls who can drop
this big man to his knees in a minute. They call him, 'Dad!'
Ken knows the greatest challenge in his life is to
give them the *Home Field Advantage.*
Full of wisdom, encouragement and practical tips from dozens
of professional athletes, this book focuses on the scoreboard
that counts most in a man's life—the health and vitality of his family.
Read it and win."

STU WEBER
AUTHOR
TENDER WARRIOR and *LOCKING ARMS*

"Ken Ruettgers has anchored the offensive line of
the Green Bay Packers for over a decade.
In his new book, Ken will give you practical tips on how you can
be that same kind of anchor for your family.
Listen to Ken's wisdom, and you will really have
a *Home Field Advantage*."

—STEVE FARRAR
PRESIDENT, MEN'S LEADERSHIP MINISTRIES
AUTHOR OF *POINT MAN*

"Ken has gathered great information along with his own
unique insights to put together
a very important book for fathers.
A very practical, interesting and vital message!"

—TIM BURKE
FATHER OF FIVE AND FORMER PITCHER
MONTREAL EXPOS

"In the *Home Field Advantage*, a most practical man
gives all of us practical advice on our own role model responsibilities.
Ken does this with much grace, in a readable, almost lyrical way.
This book is a must for men
who want to make their lives count for God where it matters most—
with their own loved ones. It is a joy to read."

—BOB BRINER
PRESIDENT OF PROSERVE TELEVISION

Home Field Advantage

MODELING YOUR LIFE WHEN THE SCORE REALLY COUNTS

KEN RUETTGERS

MULTNOMAH BOOKS
SISTERS, OREGON

HOME FIELD ADVANTAGE

published by Multnomah Books
a part of the Questar publishing family

Edited by David Kopp
Cover design by David Uttley
Cover illustration by Dan Cosgrove

International Standard Book Number: 0-88070-799-2

Printed in the United States of America

For infomration:
Questar Publishers, Inc.
Post Office Box 1720
Sisters, Oregon 97759

95 96 97 98 99 00 01 02 03 — 10 9 8 7 6 5 4 3 2 1

CONTENTS

Introduction 8

PART ONE

Undefended Territory: Confronting the role-model crisis

CHAPTER 1 *Was Charles Barkley Right?* 15
CHAPTER 2 *Beaver: 6, Beavis: 35 — Kids: 0* 31
CHAPTER 3 *Superdad to the Rescue* 49

PART TWO

Power Plays: Tackling role-model strategies

CHAPTER 4 *The Daddy Sneak* 71
CHAPTER 5 *The Triple Threat* 83
CHAPTER 6 *A Father's Arsenal* 105

PART THREE

Inside Moves: Shaping the soul of a role model

CHAPTER 7 *Working Out with God* 125
CHAPTER 8 *Exercising Your Character* 141
CHAPTER 9 *Love-Training for Marriage* 157

PART FOUR

Game Analysis: Sizing up role-model success

CHAPTER 10 *How Do I Know I'm Winning?* 181
CHAPTER 11 *When the Home Team Needs a Comeback* 195

PART FIVE

MVP Awards: Honoring role-model heroes.

CHAPTER 12 *Fathers Hall of Fame* 211
Notes 223

ACKNOWLEDGMENTS

This book wouldn't be possible without the grace and blessings of God. He placed a huge burden in my heart for children and their role models. I give Him all the glory.

I also give thanks for my wife and best friend, Sheryl. Her unconditional support and prayers helped me keep the focus on priorities during the work on this book: first God, then family, then football.

Thanks to my children, Matthew, Katherine, and Susan, for the blessing and joy they bring me. They are wonderful and unique reflections who keep their parents accountable in many ways. And thanks to my own first role models, Mom and Dad, for believing in me, putting up with me, and always being there.

God has blessed, changed, and enriched my life through several men who have had a major impact in my life: Jerry Fisher, who's been like a father to me; my Bakersfield accountability group: Steve Cabelka, Scott Pearsey, and Mike Sampley; Tunch Ilkin, the iron that keeps sharpening me; John Anderson, a roommate who put up with me, chipped away at me, and encouraged me in the Word; Tim Burke and Tom Roy—thanks for godly priorities and perspective; Steve Newman, our Packer chaplain, who has invested his life and Jesus in my life; Kent Johnston, strength coach, who keeps me strong in the weight room and in the Word; David Fitch, a gifted encourager; and Steve Farrar, a sounding board and personal inspiration.

A special thanks to Stu Weber and his family. Stu listened to me when I called out of the blue, put me in touch with Questar, and helped me throughout this process. His wife, Linda, ministered to the Packer players and wives, and sat through one of the biggest downpours of Monday Night Football with her sons Blake and Ryan—will you guys ever dry out? And thanks to Blake, who always lets me bend his ear during a busy day at Questar.

A giant thanks to all the players for their time and commitment during the interview process. I appreciate their strong stance and positive influence to families across our country. Their open hearts and transparency helped make this book unique.

During my work on this book I collected over 50 interviews from pro athletes, stacks of newspaper and magazine clippings, and 150,000 unedited words (enough material for three books). This material eventually ended up in a box at Questar Publishers. With the time-clock ticking and the book in need of an editor, the box was "hiked" into the quick and capable hands of Dave Branon. Dave worked overtime with me to transform the box into a book in a very short time. After Branon delivered a miracle, he handed off to David Kopp, editorial vice president for Questar, and his wife, Heather. They teamed up to pull the heart and soul of the role modeling issue to the surface.

A special thanks to folks at Questar. What a wonderful company of skilled and creative people. In the last few seconds of the game, these team players were able to score the final touchdown of turning a personal dream into a book.

Finally, I express thanks to the role models out there who inspire us all. Every day you continue to strive toward improvement—as godly fathers, husbands, coaches, teachers, board members. You are the power players who are changing our world by first making a difference at home.

INTRODUCTION:

GIVING SOMETHING BACK

For the last three years, my son Matthew has occasionally come to work with me. But when I take my son to my "office," it probably looks a little different than yours. That's because I work at a football stadium.

As an offensive lineman for the Green Bay Packers, my job is to play football, and my office is Lambeau Field in tradition-rich Green Bay, Wisconsin.

Matthew enjoys coming into the locker room with me and roughhousing with my teammates. I don't mind, because when he wrestles with the other players, my bruised and battered body is spared some extra wear-and-tear.

As each year passes, Matthew understands more and more about the game of football. When he first ventured with me into the locker room, he saw no difference between a superstar and a free-agent, rookie walk-on who might get cut the next day.

They were all simply "Dad's football buddies."

Big or small.

Black or white.

He didn't care. And most of my teammates treated him like he was their own son.

But during the football season after Matt turned five, he was old enough to join me on the field at the end of a game and escort the team into the locker room. And he was old enough to start figuring out just who all these guys were.

It was his first year of school. And Matt's classmates knew all about the Green Bay Packers—and which of them were the superstars. The newspapers wrote about them, the TV and radio stations talked about them, and the students' fathers seemed to place a high value on them. The kids followed suit.

The admiration was contagious, and my son caught it.

One evening during the season, after we'd won a critical game, Matt came into the locker room and asked me if I'd point him to a particular player—one of the more notable superstars on our team.

This was more than Matt simply asking about one of Dad's football buddies. It was a search for a special player.

I explained to my son where that player's locker was and told him I'd just seen the guy headed that way. After a few minutes, I went looking for Matt in that direction

There he was. But instead of playing and running around energetically as usual, he was standing dumfounded with his mouth dropped open wide. I watched him stare, speechless, seemingly caught outside some mysterious aura that surrounded the man he hoped would be his new hero.

I felt like cracking open some smelling salts to clear my head. I couldn't believe what I was seeing. Suddenly this player, who'd been just another of Dad's football buddies the year before, was in a strong position of influence.

My Green Bay Packer teammate was Matthew's new role model.

I'd watched this kind of thing happen plenty of times to someone else's son or daughter. After games or during autograph sessions, other parents' children and even some adults would approach certain Packers, too awestruck to function.

I would watch as fans stared with glassy-eyed amazement. They were actually breathing the same air as a professional athlete!

But never my son.

At least not until now.

Undetected, I watched Matt and my teammate. Anxiously waiting. Anticipating. Hoping that Matt's newfound hero would treat my son with kindness and give him just a little of his time and attention.

At the least, I hoped he'd acknowledge Matt's presence. After all, we were teammates!

At one point, the famed athlete turned from his locker and clearly saw Matt waiting to be noticed. Their eyes met.

All right, Buddy, I thought, *someone has just handed you a priceless ball.*

Do something with it. You have the power. Now is your chance to score a touch-down!

Instead, nothing happened. Zippo!

The superstar turned back to his locker. I don't know if he was too tired, had a bad day, or was just preoccupied with other thoughts.

As Matt stood watching his hero's back, I fully realized for the first time the true power, influence, and responsibility of role models. And it hit me harder than any shot I'd ever taken or delivered on the football field.

I grew up believing that athletes have a responsibility to people in society who look up to them. But the value of that role had never become real to me until my son reached out to a fellow athlete and grabbed nothing but air.

After digesting what had just happened, I took Matt's hand and walked with him back to my locker. Although we'd just won an important game, I felt the awful pain of a disappointing loss.

Matt and I sat quietly at my locker, our heads hung low as I put on shoes.

I told myself, "Boy, that guy missed an opportunity! He really fumbled the ball on that one. It would have been easy for him to score a touch-down with Matt. For a guy who has so much..."

I recalled all the great blessings the Lord had given my son's new foot-ball hero: athletic ability, good health, financial security, a great job, star status, and much more. Why hadn't my teammate—who had been given so much—responded to Matthew by giving back just a little time? Just a simple acknowledgment? A pat on the head? It would have cost him nothing.

Then a new, much more encouraging thought struck me. I knew one role model Matt could always rely on. A role model my whole family could depend on. Someone who had a running head start on being the kind of person my son needed. Someone who had a "home field advan-tage."

I'd been anxiously pointing the finger at my teammate. In essence say-ing, "I'm not the role model. You are!" I was so busy accusing my teammate of not living up to his responsibility that I failed to see who Matthew's true role model is.

Me.

I was doing what all fathers, at times, tend to do. I was waiting for someone else to help pick up the ball and run with it.

If I hadn't been waiting for my teammate, I would've been waiting for someone else. Maybe my wife or a coach. Perhaps a teacher or a grandparent. Just someone else.

Don't get me wrong. I think teachers, coaches, and many others who touch our children's lives are vital.

But when it comes to my son's life, my goal shouldn't be to hand off the role modeling task to someone else. I have the home field advantage with my children. For any of us, football players or not, our most important responsibility as a role model is at home.

Over the weeks that followed, I shared these concerns with my wife, Sheryl. She, too, recognized the importance of applying these role model principles to the home field. We prayed together for an effective way to communicate to other families how this incident with my son had affected me.

I wondered how the Lord could use my platform as a football player, working together with other Christian football players around the league, to get a positive, encouraging message out to fathers.

This book is the answer to some of those questions and prayers. It should give you a chance to reflect and re-examine your role in your family. And it will give you some practical suggestions for taking advantage of your home field position.

I think you'll enjoy the stories from the other pro athletes who contributed. Many of these stories moved me, made me laugh, and tugged at my heart. The interviewing process was a great blessing in my life, and I think you'll benefit as well.

This book allows the people we often look up to as role models to talk about how you can improve your own modeling. And it reflects the true nature of the many athletes who don't make the front pages because they don't break laws or make outlandishly self-centered statements.

This is our chance to give something positive back to football fans who support us so faithfully—to give you something that will help you be your child's favorite hero.

John 3:30

Ken Ruettgers

PART ONE

Undefended Territory: Confronting the Role-model Crisis

CHAPTER ONE

Was Charles Barkley Right?

My top role model is my dad,
because he is really big.

—JUNIOR HIGH STUDENT

It was just a shoe commercial.

A Charles Barkley shoe commercial, to be sure. And that made it worth watching for a country that has fallen in love with basketball.

But think about what we remember from that TV commercial. One thing's for certain: It's not the shoes.

It was five words. Five words that have nothing to do with footwear, yet kicked off a national debate.

"I'm not a role model," said Sir Charles into the camera.

And a nation gasped.

Barkley's statement suddenly grabbed media attention across the land as it became a hotly contested topic in homes. Those five words created the kind of controversy that cuts across political, cultural, and religious lines.

Talk shows, letters to the editor, op-ed pieces, and hundreds of magazine articles addressed Barkley's comments. It was as if another great hero had somehow let down his public, and everyone had an opinion about it.

By the start of training camp the summer after the commercial made its splash, the backlash of Charles's words had already made an impact on me.

I wasn't new to answering questions and speaking in public. For the previous eight years, I'd been a part of the Green Bay Packers' speakers' bureau. Before that, I made public appearances at the University of Southern California. I had fielded a decade-full of questions about the responsibility athletes have to the community,

But now suddenly I was getting question after question about role models. It became the topic of the month that summer for the writers covering our training camp. And the term "role model" was the new buzz-word around the locker room as the debate gathered steam.

To a collection of men who'd been looked upon as role models for years and years, this was a key question. Did we indeed have a *responsibility* as role models?

As the wrangling continued, I toyed with the idea of getting some NFL guys together to participate in a book about role models. It seemed so natural. Athletes and parents alike were trying to sort out the issue and see how it affected them and their families.

Yet I still wasn't fully convinced about the magnitude and importance of the issue—until that evening during the season when I watched my own son Matt discover the pitfalls of looking to someone other than Dad for a role model (see Introduction).

As a concerned dad and athlete, I became interested in the reaction of fellow parents who broached the subject with me. It wasn't just writers and football players who wanted to talk about Charles's seemingly heretical comment.

Other parents asked for my opinion. "Hey, Ken! What do you think of Charles Barkley's statement about not being a role model?"

I'd typically reply, "No doubt about it, I think athletes have a responsibility as role models."

Then I'd often hear a hard-edged response that worried me. "You're darned right you have a responsibility!" the parent would say.

That can make a guy in my shoes feel somewhat defensive. No one likes the finger of responsibility pointed in his or her direction — especially by parents, who are ultimately the ones responsibile for their kids. I wondered a bit about how well the finger pointers were doing in their own homes.

If the whole scenario weren't so sad, it would be funny.

Think about it. Parents point to athletes and entertainers to be role models. Athletes and entertainers respond by pointing the finger back at the parents as being the primary influencer.

The scary thing is this: If neither the parents nor the athletes are taking the responsibility as role models, then who is setting the example in our society? With all that finger-pointing going on, could anyone possibly be getting the job done properly?

As I thought carefully about the implications of what I was hearing, I decided that the key question is this: Who's going to be the role model in our own children's lives? Does it have to be an either-or proposition? How about a cooperative effort?

MEET THE REAL HEROES

In his commercial, Charles didn't stop after his first five words. He went on to say, "Parents should be role models. Just because I can dunk a basketball doesn't mean I should raise your kids."

In my limited conversations with Charles, he acknowledges that on some level athletes do indeed have a responsibility as role models. But he also feels strongly that parents must be the most important influence.

"Just because I can dunk a basketball doesn't mean I should raise your kids."

CHARLES BARKLEY
PHOENIX SUNS

I can see why this is difficult for some men to grasp. Some dads simply don't believe they're cut out to be their children's role models. Having observed famous heroes all their lives, they feel poorly equipped to compete.

They see smooth, articulate David Robinson perform on and off the court with grace and charisma, and they know they're no match for the Admiral.

They read about Reggie White and all the great things he does to help people who are in need, and they feel inadequate.

How can any dad compete with that?

NFL running back Derrick Moore understands. "No doubt athletes are looked up to, and it seems the whole globe respects them. They're blessed with talent, and they're publicized so much. Then you add the financial part, and they can really have a stronghold on kids. But having talent has nothing to do with being a role model."

The fact is, we often look at our role models and see only the exterior. We see their talent. We notice the cars they drive, the money they make, the house they live in, the fame they enjoy. We idolize them based on the outer man or woman we see.

Consider, however, what God said when the prophet Samuel visited Jesse's house to pick the next king of Israel. "Do not consider his appearance or his height.... The Lord does not look at the things man looks at. Man looks at the outward appearance, but the Lord looks at the heart" (I Samuel 16:7).

"The main influence in your child's life should not be someone whose poster hangs in their room, but someone whose life is lived out in their home."

CHARLES BARKLEY
PHOENIX SUNS

Rich or poor. Strong or weak. Articulate or mumbling. These are outward factors; God investigates the inside.

That's why it's safer if the primary influence in your child's life is not someone whose poster they have in their room, but someone whose life is lived out in their home.

Sean Jones, my teammate with the Packers, puts it bluntly and well when he says, "These are your kids. If you're not going to be a role model for your own kids, then you force them into the hands of some people who don't deserve to be looked up to."

My son, Matthew, and my daughters, Katherine and Susan, all look up to me. They think their dad is the biggest, strongest, and best dad there is. They don't think that because I possess all those traits — far from it. They don't think that way because I play football in the NFL, either.

You see dads, you're the best role models for your kids because you have the ability to be the best in their eyes. You have the ability to be their hero. If you don't follow through, someone else may try to, often unsuccessfully, and never as well as you could.

THE NUMBER ONE WAY TO LEARN

One brave basketball player who chose to respond to the Barkley brouhaha was Karl Malone. The Utah Jazz big man delivered a strong rebuttal to Barkley's commercial not long after the controversy broke.

"Charles, you can deny being a role model all you want, but I don't think it's your decision to make. We don't choose to be role models," the Mailman said. "We're chosen. Our only choice is whether to be a good role model or a bad one.

"I don't think we can accept all the glory and money that comes with being a famous athlete and not accept the responsibility of being a role model. I mean, why do we get endorsements in the first place? Because there are people who will follow our lead and buy a certain sneaker or cereal because we use it."[1]

Karl Malone doesn't believe in the "I'm not a role model" statement. Most athletes don't. They understand that if you influence someone, you are a role model.

Webster's New World Dictionary defines "role model" as, "A person so effective or inspiring in some social role, as to be a model for others." It doesn't mention the word "athlete" anywhere in the definition. It says, "a person . . . in a social role . . ." who is a "model for others."

What role could be more social than parenting? It's no coincidence that modeling is the number one way our children learn. By example. Examples they see daily.

"But you don't have to be perfect to be a good role model, and people shouldn't expect perfection," says Malone "If I were deciding whether a basketball player was a positive role model I'd want to know: Does he influence people's lives in a positive way away from the court? How much has he given of himself in time or money to help people? Does he display the values—like honesty and determination—that are part of being a good person?

HALFTIME POINTERS

Help Your Kids Find a Hero

➢ Pass on your own heroes. Was it Pete Maravich? Or John Glenn? Your kids will love to know about them. Tell why this person was your hero, what you dreamed about, how you wanted to be like him or her—and how they influenced you.

➢ Quiz your kids. List ten people you think might be your children's role models and let them rank them by preference. Include, if you're brave, yourself and a few teachers, coaches, political figures. Ask: If you had to grow up to be one of these people, who would you choose and why?

➢ Recommend Christian role models. Talk about what makes them different; for example, how they handle adversity. If your children are sports fans, here are some players you can trust:

- Basketball: A.C. Green, Mark Price, Avery Johnson, David Robinson
- Football: Reggie White, Brent Jones, Frank Reich, Guy McIntyre
- Baseball: Tim Salmon, Brett Butler, Joe Carter, Orel Hershiser
- Hockey: Mike Gartner, Adam Burt, Mark Osborne

"I do agree with Charles on one thing he says in his commercial: 'Just because I can dunk a basketball, doesn't mean I should raise your kids.' But sometimes parents need a little assistance. There are times when it helps for a mother and father to be able to say to their kids, 'Do you think Karl Malone...or David Robinson would do that?'

"Sure, parents should be role models to their children. But let's face it, kids have lots of other role models: teachers, movie stars, athletes, even other kids. As athletes, we can't take the place of parents, but we can help reinforce what they try to teach their kids."

THE SUPER STAR STANDARD

A cartoon that appeared in *USA Today* capsulizes the state of affairs from the perspective of children and their relationship to role models.

The cartoon shows a young boy and his friend in his bedroom. You can see the remnants of tape and tack holes on the walls where posters formerly hung. The boy had apparently just taken down his last poster, and you could see the name "O.J. Simpson" on it. He's telling his little friend, "That's where my Pete Rose poster was, and over there were my Darryl Strawberry and Mike Tyson posters."[2]

Our children want someone they can depend on. Someone who knows how to make the right decisions and can stand up as a good example, a light in the darkness. But in our society it's hard enough just to find people in the home who can consistently make the right decisions.

Wouldn't it be nice if we could post an ad for a role model? According to *Sports Illustrated* writer Ric Telander, it would look something like this:

> Position available: hero/role model.
> Job description: be perfect.
> Requirements: some supernatural skills, nice smile. (Suitability also may depend on an FBI check of all people applicant has come into contact with since birth).
> Hours: forever.
> Pay: none. (Outside revenue possibility: substantial) Benefits: see own face everywhere. Retirement: when scandal hits.[3]

A bit fanciful, perhaps, but it's what we want.

"Parents just have to make sure they don't take it too far," cautions Karl Malone. "Sometimes they put us on a pedestal that feels more like a tightrope—so narrow that we're bound to fall off eventually.

"This isn't something I'm especially proud of, but I've had parents in Utah say things to me like, 'You know, Karl, in our family we worship the ground you walk on. In our house your picture is right up there on the wall beside Jesus Christ.'

"Now that's going too far. Is it any wonder some athletes don't want to be role models?

"But the good things about being a role model outweigh the bad. It's a great feeling to think you're a small part of the reason that a kid decided to stay in school versus dropping out or to walk away when someone offered him drugs.

"The one thing I would encourage parents to do is to remind their kids that no matter which athletes they look up to, there are no perfect human beings. That way if the kids' heroes should make mistakes, it won't seem like the end of the world."

ASKING THE REAL QUESTION

Real-life role model Reggie Rivers of the Denver Broncos thinks he knows why people depend so much on guys like him. "As professional athletes, we're in front of a lot of people, so whether we want to be role models or not, people are going to emulate us and imitate us, especially kids.

"As long as you're in the public eye, make a lot of money, and you're a high-profile person—some people are going to think you're cool, whether you're cool or not. They're going to imitate you.

"So the question isn't whether or not you're a role model, it's whether you're a good role model or a bad role model."

Long before Reggie Rivers had an inkling that he'd become a professional football player and a role model for thousands of young people, he learned how a bad role model could affect his life.

"I must have been nine or ten years old," Rivers recalls. "I was playing on a basketball team, and I think I was the best player on the team. That wasn't always the case when I was growing up, but on this particular team it was.

"I remember one game where I kept getting called for fouls. I had three fouls, then four, and eventually I fouled out. It was the first time I'd ever fouled out of a game, so I wasn't sure how to act.

"When I got my fifth foul, I stamped my foot on the floor and went marching over to the bench.

"I knew I was the best player on this team, and I thought that's how the best player is supposed to act. I sat there on the bench with a towel around my neck and didn't cheer for anybody.

"I'd seen the guys on the TV—the prima donna players. I noticed they acted like they should be mad to be out of the game. They wanted people to think that they'd never be content on the bench.

"After the game, I got in the car with my dad and he said, 'You know, Reggie, I was so embarrassed of you tonight.'

"He'd been sitting up there in the stands watching me play, and there was a man sitting next to him. As the game went along, this man kept telling my dad, 'You know, that Reggie is a heck of a good player, and he always keeps his cool and has a good attitude.'

"'Then,' my dad told me, 'you get that fifth foul.... I was embarrassed because that's not like you. That's not the kind of person I think you are, and I don't think that's the kind of person you want to be.'

"I was just a kid, but that's something I remember to this day in the way I carry myself, particularly when I'm on the field. I don't ever want people to think I'm a prima donna."

We all see these negative examples as we watch games and read the sports pages. Often it's these images that capture the imagination of the fans. An ounce of negative influence seems to outweigh 10 pounds of positive influence.

Just look at the difficulty major league baseball is having as it tries to restore its good name. Here's an institution that's been around for more than 100 years, has amassed the greatest traditions in American sports, and even has the corner on the title "American pastime."

And yet, a strike that disrupted two seasons and cost fans the World Series has soured many on the game. Whether the strike was justified or not, the negative impact of the walkout tarnished the positive reputation of baseball—and its players.

But then, athletes have never been as perfect as their images. Remember the lifestyles that baseball and football players led in the '40's and '50's? Who could forget the stories of Babe Ruth and his wild trips to the bars? In the movie, *Eight Men Out,* the Chicago White Sox are shown throwing the World Series in 1919. In the same film, a disillusioned young fan says to Joe Jackson, "Shoeless Joe, say it ain't so."

Human failure is a factor that makes the issue of role models a slippery one. Like so many other areas of society, we prefer easy solutions in the face of complex questions. We'd like to think our sports heroes are exempt from the flaws of humanity, but it ain't so.

Nevertheless, as a professional athlete who knows how players think, I can vouch for many pros who are positively influencing our society. I agree with Paul Attner, who wrote in *The Sporting News*, "This generation of pro athletes is the most generous and giving in history by far. Surprise you? It shouldn't."[4]

Sports attorney Leigh Steinberg and his partner Jeff Moorad believe in a philosophy of positive influence and giving back to the community. They encourage the athletes they represent to embrace these ideals as well.

"The public is presented with a distorted image of athletic behavior off the field," Steinberg says. "It's a disservice. We are given a heavy dose of news about athletes who drink, use drugs, or misbehave, and we aren't told about the vast majority who do their jobs, drive home after work, eat with their families, and give back to the community. That's not news, but it's the accurate image of our athletes."

This emphasis on what critics call the "negative obsession" of news reporting is a sad part of the sports story. Perhaps it's up to fans and players to keep the negative examples from edging out the good ones. If we don't, we could end up in a world without role models.

A WORLD WITHOUT ROLE MODELS—WHAT IF?

What would that kind of world look like? What would it feel like? What would it be like if our nation's leaders from the President on down all decided to shirk the responsibility of being a positive role model? The story of our land might read like this:

In a world without positive role models, movie stars and rock and role stars would die of drug overdoses, and committing acts of immorality would be socially acceptable.

The most interesting stories about our sports stars would not be found in the sports section—they would dominate the news that is usually reserved for criminal activities.

Citizens would expect and accept the lies, adulterous acts, and cover-ups of politicians as they continued to bend and break the laws they were voted to uphold

The clergy would fall regularly from the pulpit. Police would take bribes and unnecessarily beat people in the streets. They would look the other way as crimes were being committed.

Insurance fraud cases would escalate, and the rate of rapes, muggings, and murders would skyrocket. Stock and security brokers would embezzle millions of dollars.

Schoolyards would no longer be safe for our children, and violent riots would destroy hundreds of acres of city communities. Street gangs would control the neighborhoods and hold our families hostage.

Single-parent households would be the accepted norm as fathers would run away from their role in the home. Authority figures would live by the "do as I say, not as I do" rule.

Children would grow up following the examples set by people who have no regard for civility, etiquette, morality, honor, love, charity, or righteousness.

Scary? Absolutely! What's even more scary is that you can reread those paragraphs and see the influences that are actually at work on our children. Except for the exaggeration, this scenario sounds very much like America today.

IN SEARCH OF INFLUENCE

Sadly, there are kids everywhere crying out for the kind of examples that would be missing from a role-model-free society. They need someone in their lives because the person who should be there for them isn't.

Single mothers are begging for role models for their sons and daughters.

Families are looking for role models to be examples of character for their children as they grow up facing tough, real-life issues, pressures, and decisions.

Business and professional men and women are searching for legitimate leadership that will model professional ethics in the middle of an environment that looks first at its bottom line. Citizens behind our country's political grassroots movement are angrily expressing the need for ethics and moral leadership among our elected officials.

Almost all ethnic groups are looking hard for examples of leadership to exemplify quality values, morals, and character in a mixed-up world. In a big way, our society is yearning for proper influence by legitimate role models of noble character.

Thousands of young people are growing up without familial role models in their lives. One of them is Edward Williams, a young hero-worshipper profiled in *Sporting News.*

"Edward, 16, attends high school in St. Louis and lives in one of the city's toughest neighborhoods. An all-around athlete, he's developed his sports skills at Matthews-Dickey Boy's Club, which services most of the inner city youths.

"He'd like to play linebacker in the pros, and his sports hero is Bills linebacker Cornelius Bennett. Williams talks about athletic role models and his relationship with sports.

"'I'd like to see pros come to Matthews-Dickey once in a while and give speeches that would help teenagers stay out of trouble and keep away from stuff like drugs. I've seen some messages on television talking about football camps, but not about drugs.

"'It would be a big influence to have them here in person. If Cornelius Bennett was doing the talking, man, would it be something! He's been my role model since I was little, and I would do what he said to do, because he's been so successful and it's worked for him.

"'It's bad out there. I live in just about the worst neighborhood in St. Louis. I've been offered drugs, guns, everything. We have just about the biggest population of Bloods, a gang, in Missouri, near here. It's hard to get away from them. They're trying to influence me. They want me to hang with them. They don't go to school or anything, but I had an uncle who started off selling drugs at 13. He was with a gang. He has been in jail six or seven times, and he's not getting anywhere.

"'If I could talk to the pros, I would tell them to stop fighting in games. They really influence kids by doing that. Kids see it, and think they can do it, because the people who are doing it are so good, why can't kids do it too?

"'I used to love the Detroit Pistons and Bill Laimbeer, even though just about every other guy hated him. Then he got in a fight with his own teammate. I didn't pay attention to him anymore after that. Why would he act that way?'"[5]

GIVE YOUR KIDS SOME CREDIT

Young Edward just brought up an important point. Kids do care about their role-models' behavior. Children have their own set of standards and often they will apply them—even to the superhero who's captured their heart.

Fact is, most kids don't necessarily want to emulate *all* of a hero's qualities. They admire the talent being displayed. That's what they hope to imitate.

Our job is to help them differentiate those qualities, good and bad, right from the start. You can tell a child, "This is not a good guy to follow." But you do a better job if you *help* your child come to his own good conclusions.

If your children like a star whose habits or lifestyle you question, rather than order your children to dump the star immediately (good luck!), see if you can't get a good discussion going.

As you talk, give your children credit on the front end for the reasons they admire Joe Drug-Addict-Jock. But then go on to ask about his morals. What do your children think about such behavior? Ponder together why a person with so much going for him might choose a destructive, unhappy way of life.

It also doesn't hurt to track with your children's heroes yourself—in the paper and through the media—and keep the discussion going.

You can, by the way, put your foot down on certain promotional items such as posters, videos, or music that are particularly immoral or offensive in nature. If you're lucky, your children might agree. If not, stick to your guns.

A good way to handle this might be to buy a new poster or CD to replace the objectionable one. Perhaps you can pick it out together with your children.

Finally, do some brainstorming in your children's areas of interest. It never hurts to make suggestions for new role models. Introduce your kids to amazing people they might admire if they knew more about them.

By the way, do your kids know who you admire—and why?

WELCOME TO YOUR HOME FIELD ADVANTAGE

By now, I think the point has been well made. America needs role models, and athletes can serve admirably in that role. It's not a system of volunteers. It's a draft. As athletes, we have no choice.

But we're not alone. What we are doing should be supplementary to the role modeling that goes on at home.

I can't say it any better than Karl Malone when he observed, "It's how athletes, fathers, mothers, family members, friends, and neighbors respond to the challenge of being chosen as a role model that makes the difference in the lives of children.

"I can't think of any person closer to children than their parents. No other role model has the ability to influence on a daily basis through good example as often as parents."

No other role model has the home field advantage.

One of the most outstanding young players in the NFL in 1994 was Cris Carter of the Minnesota Vikings.

"I have a little boy and a daughter," said the talented tight end, "and the number one role model for them is me. If they happen to pick up some role models along the way, they'll be secondary to the course or direction of their life that I have given them, because I spend more time with them than anybody.

"I don't know how parents can plan on somebody else being a role model for their kids when, for the most part, they've never met these people. It's the parents who spend the time with their kids.

"...When you try to have other role models, especially Christians, you need to be very careful. Understand that they're human, and the human side of them will disappoint you. But you shouldn't let that take your sights off of the ultimate role model, Jesus."

Leave it to another offensive lineman, San Francisco's Steve Wallace, to echo these thoughts. "The role model should be the parents at home. A lot of times we as players may go somewhere, and a parent who is having trouble with a kid will say, 'Can you talk to little Johnny?'

"And I say, 'Yeah, I can talk to him, but at the same time, you can do a lot more than I can do.'

"It won't hurt me to spend time talking to Johnny about the things it takes to succeed, but the most important thing is that the parent has to accept the responsibility.

"I'm going to give my time as far as helping out, but I know that my biggest responsibility is at home with my girls. I can't expect them to be led by somebody they can't even see, meet, or touch. It has to be me."

So, where have we gone with this debate that Mr. Barkley sparked while selling shoes? In effect, we've gone back to his words. We've seen that he perhaps understated the importance of his part in the role model drama, for indeed as an athlete he does affect young lives by the millions.

But we've also seen that it's not the millions that are the issue. It is the one, two, three, four, or however many children God has given each dad. They are the ones who need a special role model. They need someone who can play ball with them, not just play ball in front of them.

They need a role model who can sit down and dialogue with them, not just present a monologue on a thirty-second TV commercial.

They need someone to model the spiritual disciplines that will make it possible for them to grow to be more like Jesus Christ.

They need a shining model of strong character and ethical purity.

They need a man who will love, nurture, and prize their mother.

They need a dad who can give them a game plan for life.

"Kids need someone who can play ball with them, not just play ball in front of them."

CHARLES BARKLEY
PHOENIX SUNS

How has the role modeling been in your life? Are you like the parents who think I'll do the modeling for their kids because I play football? Or are you more like the football players I quoted who know that life is not a game?

The phrase "I'm not a role model" doesn't work for Charles Barkley, and it won't work for you, either. Together, let's look at how we can become the dads we really want to be.

PERSONAL TIME-OUT

1. Who have been some of my favorite role models over the years? What characteristics did I admire in them? Can my children see some of those characteristics in me?

2. What part do I think role models play in my children's lives? When was the last time I discussed with them who their models were and why?

3. What would I do if my children told me their role model was someone like Madonna?

4. What are some things I can teach my children in the next two weeks through better role modeling?

CHAPTER TWO

Beaver: 6, Beavis: 35 —Kids: 0

My dad is my role model because he is hard-working and not a quitter. He has shown me how to work hard and achieve my goals.

—THIRTEEN-YEAR-OLD BOY

Some of the most violent hits in the NFL happen when a player gets blindsided. It's such a vicious hit because the player never sees it coming.

Just watch highlight tapes from NFL Films. You cringe as a wide receiver leaps to catch the ball, only to get knocked upside down and spun around like a rag doll. Often he goes one way, the ball goes another, and his helmet goes flying in still another direction.

It's a violent event in a violent sport, and it happens to every player. It's happened to me several times.

I can still remember one such hit. It was a perfect October day for football in Green Bay, and we were hosting the Vikings. The temperature was in the low sixties and our attendance was in the high fifties—it was another sellout.

We were battling the Vikings toe-to-toe, and late in the third quarter the game could still go either way. The sun had begun to fall below the top of the stadium, creating a bright spot for anyone facing that direction.

We had the ball on the Vikings' 30, and we were threatening to score and take the lead. Our quarterback dropped back into the pocket to throw. As he did, the sun's glare blocked his vision, and he fired the ball blindly in the direction of the receiver. The ball was tipped right into the hands of the defender. The Vikings had intercepted.

Now, as much as I hate to see our quarterback throw an interception, as an offensive lineman, there's one thing about it that gets me excited. I get a chance to nail the guy who intercepted my teammate's pass. There are few things more fun than exploding through a hit and manhandling this thief.

Besides, we often outweigh defensive backs by one hundred pounds. It's a chance to pick a target, pin your ears back, and let it all go. Kamikaze style.

And if that's not enough incentive, it gives us offensive linemen the chance to rack up a positive statistic: a tackle. Most often, the stats we earn are negative points for giving up sacks or racking up a penalty.

When the Viking guy picked off my mate's pass, I was in great position to lower the boom. I honed in on his numbers, and I was thinking about nothing but bringing him down.

It would be the hit of the game. I could taste it. An NFL Films highlight in the making. ESPN would be replaying the hit across the entire nation later that night. My old high school friends would be so proud of me.

But then it happened. I was blindsided. Out of nowhere came a flying Viking with my ear hole in his sights. He hit me so hard that he knocked me off my feet. As I went airborne, I crashed into Greg Feasel, my fellow tackle—a man who outweighs me by twenty pounds. He, too, went down.

Greg was ticked. He looked at me as we lay sprawled on the turf and demanded to know why I'd kept him from getting in on the tackle. When I told him that I'd been blindsided, he wanted to know what freight train had just knocked 590 pounds of beef to the ground.

After I regained my senses, I realized that it was one of those little defensive backs who'd sent us both into next week. I couldn't believe it. A defensive back! One of the smallest guys on the field.

Now he would be on the ESPN highlight tape, and I never even saw him coming.

I learned that day that it helps to keep your head on a swivel. When your head's on a swivel, your vision improves because you're looking all around you, carefully scouting out any incoming attacks. You can anticipate the hit—and avoid it or make it less effective. Vision is the key to not being blindsided.

I can't help but think that our entire society has been blindsided over the past thirty years. And apparently, we weren't looking, and we got hit so hard by new ways of thinking, new lifestyle choices, and a new morality that we've been knocked to the ground.

Let's look at what hit this society. And let's see what we, as dads, can do to force a turnover.

TALE OF TWO SHOWS

One good way to show how our nation's values and morals have changed over the past thirty years is to look at two famous TV characters: The Beaver and Beavis.

Beaver Cleaver of *Leave It To Beaver* was no angel, of course. He would mess up his brother Wally's sport coat or break a window here and there. But he was always acting in the innocent naiveté of childhood. He meant no real harm, and none was ever done.

More important, Beaver's indiscretions always led him to an inevitable showdown with his warm but firm dad, Ward. In today's world, the entire concept of *Leave It To Beaver* is criticized and mocked for its cut-and-dried morality. It's called square, unrealistic, and banal.

Those unfair characterizations aside, the program represented something basic and right in our society. It showed that families can exist in a favorable climate. Sure, it was a bit idealistic. There is no program on TV that portrays life exactly as it is.

Today, however, the kind of kids who laughed innocently along with the Beav and Wally are exchanging the guttural, sneering laugh of a far different character. His name is Beavis, and he epitomizes all that could possibly be wrong with a young person.

This is no portrayal of innocent naiveté. It is blatant rebellion, crass disrespect for authority, clear rejection of moral standards, shameless glorification of sexual immorality, gross indecency, and an open invitation to no-holds-barred hedonism.

In case you don't get the idea: In one episode, Beavis and his cohort, Butthead, are invited to a friend's house to check out his new video game. Instead, they "get happy" with the gas stove. And then they light a match. The whole kitchen blows up.

Did they call 911? Not on your life, folks.

Did they use the fire-extinguisher displayed nearby?

Naah. That was just for effect.

This was funny. Maybe you had to be there. Then again, maybe even that wouldn't have helped.

WHAT HAPPENED TO AMERICA?

In a July 1994 *American Legion* magazine article called "What Went Wrong With our Country?" Gary Bauer, director of the Family Research Council, tells us, "Last year I heard a story about a California school teacher. She had taught many years ago, and then went home to raise her children. Just recently she went back to teaching.

"A generation ago, she said, she would enter the classroom and say, 'Good morning, students,' and they would reply, 'Good morning, Mrs. Jones.'

"When she returned to the classroom in 1993, she said, 'Good morning, students,' and one of them yelled back, 'Shut up, b—,' and everybody laughed. The teacher asked this question, 'What happened to America between "Good morning, Mrs. Jones," and "Shut up, b—"? When did that happen? And what are we going to do about it?'"

WE GOT USED TO LOSING

One person who is trying to answer those kinds of questions is William Bennett, former secretary of education. He has done extensive research into the cause of the decline of morality in America, and he has created a system for charting that decline.

His system is called the Index of Leading Cultural Indicators. In a winter 1994 *Policy Review* article titled "Revolt Against God," Bennett summarized a speech given at the twentieth anniversary of the Heritage Foundation. In that speech Bennett reviewed some of the results of his index, which he called, "The most comprehensive statistical portrait available of behavioral trends over the last thirty years.

"There's been a 560-percent increase in violent crime, more than a 400-percent increase in illegitimate births, a quadrupling in divorces, and a tripling of the percentage of children living in single-parent homes; more than a 200-percent increase in the teenage suicide rate, and a drop of 75 points in the average SAT scores of high school students."

Later in the article, Bennett wrote, "Consider too, where the United States ranks in comparison to the rest of the industrial world. We are at, or near, the top in rates of abortions, divorces, and unwed births. We lead the industrialized world in murder, rape, and violent crime, yet in elementary and secondary education, we are at, or near, the bottom in achievement scores.

"I don't think we are angry enough."

WILLIAM BENNETT
FORMER SECRETARY OF EDUCATION

"These facts alone are evidence of substantial social regression," Bennett concluded. "This may sound overly pessimistic, or even alarmist, but I think this is the way it is, and my worry is that people are not unsettled enough. We have become inured to the culture rot that is setting in. We are getting used to it, even though it's not a good thing to get used to.

"A few weeks ago, eleven people were murdered in New York City within ten hours, and as far as I can tell, it barely caused a stir. Two weeks ago, a violent criminal, who mugged and almost killed a 72-year-old man, and who was shot by a police officer while fleeing the scene of the crime, was awarded 4.3 million. Silence. Virtual silence.

"'We are defining deviancy down,' says Senator [Patrick] Moynihan, 'and in the process, we are losing a once reliable sense of civic and moral outrage.'"

Perhaps Bennett's quote of author John Updike best describes what America has done to itself. "The fact that we still live well cannot ease the pain of feeling that we no longer live nobly," Updike said.

In his article, Bennett gave some examples of a country that has lost its outrage.

HALFTIME POINTERS

TV Strategies that Score

➢ "Unplug your kids." Take your kids off from the TV completely for a few days—let them get bored. They may need time to relearn how to entertain themselves.

➢ Have the guts to disagree with neighbors or friends on what's okay viewing and what's not. If you have to walk out of a movie, do it. Tell your kids to always consult you about what they watch at a friend's.

➢ Set limits. Sheryl and I allow some viewing because we think if kids are never allowed to watch anything, they become unduly curious, creating an even bigger problem. We say, go for balance.

➢ Practice as a family judging if a show is okay. Try these guidelines:

- Is this show age-appropriate for your kids?
- Is this good language to hear?
- Who's portrayed as heroes: good guys or bad guys?
- How will the show help you make good choices?
- How about trigger points: profanity, sex, nudity, violence?

"Listen to the story from former New York City Police Commissioner Norman Kelley. 'A number of years ago, there began to appear in the windows of automobiles parked on the streets of American cities signs which read: "No radio." Rather than expressing outrage or even annoyance at the possibility of a car break-in, people tried to communicate with the potential thief in conciliatory terms. The translation of "No radio" is: "Please, break into someone else's car. There's nothing in mine."'

"These signs are flags of urban surrender. They are handwritten capitulations. Instead of 'No radio,' we need new signs that say, 'No surrender.'"

Bennett continued, "It is hard to remember now, but there was once a time when personal failures, subliminal desires, and perverse taste were accompanied by guilt or embarrassment. At least by silence. Today, these are a ticket to appear as a guest on *The Sally Jessie Raphael Show,* or one of the dozen or so shows like it."

To prove his point, Bennett relayed a variety of subjects that appeared on daytime talk shows, as compiled by Bennett's staff. The programs featured cross-dressing couples, a three-way love affair, a man whose chief aim in life is to sleep with women and fool them into thinking that he is using a condom during sex, women who can't say no to cheating, prostitutes who love their jobs, a former drug dealer, an interview with a young girl caught in the middle of a bitter custody battle.

"These shows," Bennett concluded, "present a two-edge problem to society. The first edge is that some people want to appear on these shows in order to expose themselves. The second edge is that lots of people are tuning in to watch them expose themselves."

Beyond Bennett's findings, it's not hard to find many other examples of how our modern society has lost its bearings.

What many years ago used to result in major headlines on the front page in every major newspaper across the country is now but a blurb, lost to the numbing realities of mass murders, bombings, parent killings, and so forth.

But it's not just murders and bodily attacks that have been on the increase. There are a multitude of other moral indiscretions that have awakened us to the fact that the problems of our society are widespread.

A FAILURE OF ETHICS

In 1993 the Family Research Council conducted a poll of changing American values. According to Gary Bauer, the poll revealed that 72 percent of Americans believe that changes in family life over the past three decades "have been generally for the worst."

In 1990, the Josephson Institute of Ethics in California released a synthesis of studies on the ethics of contemporary youth. That survey revealed that some 75 percent of high school students admitted to cheating at one time or another, as did 50 percent of college students.

SELF-CENTEREDNESS

In a TV commercial I saw not long ago, actress Cindy Crawford announced, "Isn't it time you got what you deserve?"

To me, it summed up where our society is. We're a society that feels as if we deserve everything given to us, and we deserve it right now. We've become obsessed with claiming what we believe to be ours, and we're very impatient.

This alone is a complete and significant change from our society even thirty years ago.

LAZINESS

Tunch Ilkin, a fine NFL linebacker for many years, noticed a change in the attitude of his teammates when he went from one team to another.

"In Pittsburgh," Tunch declared, "guys don't even train anymore. They don't watch as much film. The young guys put no emphasis or premium on lifting weights. All they do is want to show off and do their thing. The attitude is, 'So why should I watch any film? What's that going to tell me? How's that going to make me a better ball player?'

"That whole attitude just blows me away. I don't know if it's the money or this time in history."

Ilkin sees the same thing away from the football field. "When I contract out a job," he said, "if I'm looking for someone to do stonework or I'm putting a new sidewalk in, it's hard for me to hire someone who is young. I always look for a guy older than me, because they usually have a better work ethic. They take a lot of pride in a job well done.

"I think our generation is such an 'I, I, I, me, me, me, I expect, I expect' generation, that it doesn't take pride in its work. They just say, 'I want to get my money, I want to get the job done, I want to go on.'"

But why is this? Tunch has an opinion: "I think that we've gotten to be such a godless society that there are no absolutes any more. If you don't live with an eternal perspective, that you're going to be held accountable, then why not cheat, why not be lazy?

"If you live by the standards God has set for us, then you can't be lazy. God says, 'That's not what I want from you, I want your best effort. I don't care if you're great, I don't care if you stink, but I want your best effort. I did my best for you, so I want your best in return.'"

ARROGANCE

Another fellow football player, teammate Guy McIntyre, has a similar feeling about the changes in people over the years. "The old guys used to bring the young guys in and they'd be willing to follow the older guys' example. It just made for a better team.

"But I think it's different today. These guys come out of college, and they think they know all there is to know. I think with the money they make nowadays, it kind of gives them the rite of passage without even going through a training camp or a whole season.

"Of course, there are some who do listen and do seek advice and follow the examples of others."

DEVIANCE

Sure, we've always had people with odd ideas about things. But more and more, today's aberrant ideas on topics of fundamental concern are being listened to by policy makers and the media.

The rearrangement of America's thinking on the family has opened the door to a wide and weird array of strange ideas.

In "What's Shere Hite's Beef About the Family?" an article that appeared in the September 1994 issue of *Chatelaine,* feminist Hite calls into question some of the basics of the traditional family.

"Those people who have made family values their cry are really promoting fascist values, a hierarchy of discipline and obedience." Hite goes on to say, "Why assume that humans are flawed and that the family structure is fine and good if so many are finding that they can't fit into it?"

She urges the development of diverse and new kinds of families, not matriarchal, but rather democratic, with an equal voice for each man, woman, and child. She also praises the benefits of single-parent families and families raised by same gender couples.

Peggy O'Mara, of the same ilk as Hite, had a similarly odd revelation. O'Mara, editor of *Mothering,* was quoted from the summer 1991 issue of her magazine as saying, "The family is dead and it is a good thing."

I wonder what she would conclude if she were to drop by my house and see my wife and I interacting with our children? Or if she were to visit the other millions of families across this continent. Yet people who continue to say such ridiculous things are given a forum and a following in this society.

Dr. James Dobson has a good twist on this phenomenon. "Though we exist by graciousness of a loving Lord," he said, "humanity is systematically seeking to overthrow him as the moral authority of the universe. We jettison his commandments and replace them with our puny notions and ideas. Secular humanism has concluded that there are no eternal truths, no transcendent values, no ultimate rights and wrongs.

"What seems right at the time is right. Morality is determined by public opinion polls as though our pooled ignorance will somehow produce variety. In the process we have forgotten the faith of our fathers that was lovingly handed down to us and entrusted to our care."[1]

THE BOX THAT ATE AMERICA

About forty years ago, a new force was unleashing itself on the land. Oh, it was harmless enough at first—what with its quaint presentations of *I Love Lucy* and Ed Sullivan. But television has grown up from its tiny beginnings inside a sturdy wooden box in the corner of a few living rooms to become The Box that Ate America.

Television—along with its older ancestors, movies and radio, as well as its younger cousins, VCRs, tapes, CDs, and the information superhighway—has played a vital role in the rearrangement of American culture.

Even though TV producers are willing to pick any disgusting topic they can find to show on their programs, they have a clear prejudice against one scary topic.

George W. Cornell, writing for the Associated Press, quoted Bill Moyers, who observed, "Just about every other human endeavor is the subject of continuing coverage by the media, even to the point of saturation. Economics, politics and government business, foreign policies, sports, sex, cooking, consumer interest, physical fitness, movies and entertainment, war, crime, even wrestling.

"But there is no room at the inn for religion as a crucial force in American life. So most Americans remain religiously illiterate."[2]

Why the boycott? Why are the media moguls so afraid of a belief in God and a trust in religious worship—something that more than ninety percent of Americans embrace as a key element in the founding of our country? Why does religion continue to be the only subject absent from TV as art imitating life?

This neglect of the divine leaves Americans who spend much time watching TV with a twisted view of life—one that says there's nothing important about faith.

No wonder some of our priorities are not quite right in regard to how valuable we've made the media and its components. Consider that in a recent year, Americans spent $1.7 billion on Nintendo products—the exact amount that was spent by American churches on world missions.[3]

CAPTURING A WHOLE NEW GENERATION

Now a whole new generation of Americans is being blindsided. It's the MTV generation, and they're so much more media-oriented than my age group that there's a danger we won't even be able to communicate with them. They are the generation that was born with a remote control in their hand.

These kids are being blindsided by a media culture that, as pointed out above, refuses to recognize the importance of faith in American life. But even worse, it is in many ways anti-God and promotes ideas that run contrary to biblical truth. A generation growing up on this doesn't know it's being taught lies that lead to destruction.

Often the purveyors of today's media presentations will contend that they really have no effect on young people, that they're just entertaining them. The facts prove differently.

Take, for example, a story reported in *Media Update*. "A young man in Natchez, Mississippi, was seriously injured this year after falling off a water tower. He was trying to paint the message 'Billy Bo Bob loves Charlene' on the tower. He told reporters he was influenced by a country music hit by Joe Diffie called John Deere Green, in which a boy climbs a water tower and paints a heart on it.

"Diffie apologetically pleaded with the people not to climb water towers, saying that was not the intent of his song."

That tragedy happened through the influence of someone who seems to care that his song had a negative impact. Imagine what's happening through the uncaring influence of the many star performers who blatantly desire to tear down the morals of their listeners.

Janet Jackson, whose concert tours criss-cross the nation with her new, sexually liberating music and stage show, had this to say in Rolling Stone, "I love doing deeply sexual music and I don't mind letting the world know."[4]

Shortly after this, in an MTV rockumentary interview, Janet said, "When you put out an album, and people say, 'That album changed my life,' that does make you a role model, whether you want to be or not."

Imagine the effect this role model's "deeply sexual" music has on teenagers who can't wait to follow her lead.

And then there's rapper Easy E. When a reporter for the *Los Angeles Times* asked him how a rapper's legal troubles would affect his career, he said, "It gets blurred up even more, but it's good for record sales to be on the cover of *Time* magazine and all that. That's good for record sales. If you can sell four million records off shooting somebody, I'd say you can beat that case."[5]

If we think as parents that we can counteract these kinds of influences with a simple word of caution, we may find that we are faced with a problem far greater than we understand. Part of the entire thrust of much of what today's kids hear is set up to make sure our influence on them is negated. Michael Medved put it like this:

"In addition to its relentless anti-marriage message that undermines the connection between husbands and wives, the popular culture also helps to poison relationships between parents and children. No notion has been more aggressively and ubiquitously promoted in films, popular music and television than the idea that children know best, that parents are corrupt, hypocritical clowns who must learn decency and integrity from their enlightened offspring."[6]

And if we are under the illusion that this kind of message is not being heard by church kids, we need to consider this: "A surprising study by Barna Research Group reveals that Christian baby busters would be more likely to have watched MTV during the past week.

"The totals were 42 percent compared with 33 percent of their non-Christian counter parts."[7]

Author Steve Farrar has said that letting our kids watch the wrong TV is like letting them drink contaminated water out of the toilets or gutters. He's not too far off.

WHO OR WHAT WILL INSPIRE A REBOUND?

When a football team runs into a slump, they can do one of two things: They can pack it in for the year and give up. Or they can go back to the playbook, rethink their strategy, redouble their efforts, and dig in for the long haul.

I'm a believer in the second strategy. Giving up and giving in is simply not on my list of possibilities.

That's why all of these bad statistics and stories that we've just waded through don't scare me. Remember, I've decided not to get blindsided anymore. So I'm looking for solutions that will lead us out of the cultural abyss we've gotten knocked into.

But who should we call onto the field?

THE GOVERNMENT OR OTHER INSTITUTIONS?

Many Americans look to some faraway institution to solve the problems that perplex our land. It could be the schools. It could be the Congress. It could be the president.

Yet we must understand that if our crisis is moral, we can't depend on institutions that don't promote morality as the Bible describes it.

A good example is how government seeks to answer two of the great moral crises in our land: teenage pregnancy and the increase in sexually transmitted diseases.

According to Rush Limbaugh, the government-run schools of America's largest city are attacking the problem. See if you think this is any kind of solution: "Of course we know many school districts are teaching kids about so-called safe sex techniques and distributing condoms. Here are some things excerpted directly from so-called educational material currently being distributed in the school system of New York.

"The Teenagers Bill of Rights: 'I have the right to decide whether to have sex and who to have it with. I have the right to use protection when I have sex. I have the right to buy and use condoms.

"'Condoms can be sexy. They come in different colors, sizes, flavors and styles to be more fun for you and your partner. You can put them on together. Shop around until you find the type you like best. Be creative and be safe...guys can get used to the feel of condoms while masturbating.'"[8]

We all know what the results of this kind of teaching will be. And we know that it won't have anything remotely to do with biblical morality.

A Spiritual Reawakening?

Former drug czar and current values guardian William Bennett knows from experience that the education system won't stop the moral slide in America. He recognizes the spiritual dimension to the solution.

"What afflicts us is a corruption of the heart, a turning away in the soul. Our aspirations, our affections, and our desires are turned toward the wrong things, and only when we turn them toward the right things—toward enduring, noble, spiritual things—will things get better.

"Today, we must decline to accept the end of moral man. We must carry on the struggle for our children. We will push back hard against an age that is pushing hard against us. When we do, we will emerge victorious against the trials of our time. When we do, we will save our children from the decadence of our time. We have lots of work to do. Let's get to it."

An Army of Dedicated Dads?

William Bennett is talking to us, dads. He is talking to the major role model for our children and for our wives. He is calling us to action. It's the parents of America who have the resources to rescue this society.

If you still need marching orders, listen to author Steve Farrar. "A man who's going to ride for the brand and fight the good fight must, along with his wife, discern his culture, defend his convictions, disciple his children."

"What many men don't realize," Farrar wrote later in his book, "is that someone or something is leading your family. Now, is it you, or is it your television? Is it you, or the peers of your children? Make no mistake, someone is leading. Do you know who that someone or something is?"[9]

We dads have a job to do, and we can begin to take on the challenge in our own home, but there's another consideration. Our country, because of its past mistakes, has millions of young people who don't have a father to look up to, or if they do, he isn't someone with the moral fortitude to guide them.

One fellow football player with a passion for that type of child is Ray Seals of the Pittsburgh Steelers.

"There's a lot of kids in the inner city where there's not a father around. They're not with families. There just has to be more role models out there to work with them.

"But if some people would move down into the inner city, maybe not in the thick of things, but where you see them every day and relate, they would get a whole different view of what's going on down there.

"Spend more time down in those areas. Instead of driving down and locking your doors, spend some time at functions and Boys' Clubs and the YMCA. Become involved. It might change a lot of points of view in the way people think, if they see it first hand."

This is a heavy responsibility for all of us as dads to think about, no matter what color our skin is or what church we go to. Jesus wants us to spread the gospel to the ends of the world, but we've got representatives from all nations right in our backyards that we're flying over.

And we've got our own family, too. Right in our backyards.

Maybe the bad news in this chapter makes you feel as if you've got poor field position as a father. In some ways, that's true. But because of your teaching and role modeling, your kids won't be blindsided. We really can change our world for the better, one kid at a time.

PERSONAL TIME-OUT

1. Am I really convinced that what the media conveys is all that bad? What does it convey that's good?

How could I appy Philippians 4:8–9 to an evening of TV viewing to see how it lines up with Paul's criteria for what to think about?

2. What changes have I noticed in society over the past couple of decades? What have I done to stop the slide in my life or in the lives of my children?

3. How do I know if my children are being affected by the TV—at home or away?

4. When my children see how I use the media, do they see a balanced role model? Why?

5. Has my family ever done anything to help those who are not as fortunate as we are? What can we do in the next month to share with them our wealth and our faith?

RUETTGERS' REFLECTIONS

Football truths that also work in real life

Always protect your inside; it's the quickest way to the quarterback.

We're not letting the inmates run the prison. —Offensive line coach.

Don't get overconfident when things are going well. That is the time to tighten down the screws.

Know your opponents' strengths and weaknesses.

To be good and to last, you have to know when to turn it on and when to turn it off.

CHAPTER THREE

Superdad to the Rescue

My father helps me to accomplish what I want.
He made me into what I am

—FOURTEEN-YEAR-OLD BOY

Offensive linemen are a breed apart in the world of football. We're the crucial element of any successful offense. But we have a different outlook on things than the high-profile players such as quarterbacks, running backs, and receivers.

Those position players get most of the glory and a lot of the attention.

We get the joy of protecting the stars—down after down after down without anybody making much of a fuss over us. Unless we get called for a penalty or give up a QB sack, we go pretty much unnoticed by the guys in the broadcasting booth. We accumulate no yards, no receptions, and no touchdowns.

Yet we've done exactly what we were supposed to do.

Blair Bush, a first-round draft pick at center, and a player who toiled for fifteen years in the NFL, once told me that the secret to being an offensive lineman is to go unnoticed.

Do you know the name Blair Bush? Probably not. So it seems that he was right.

Maybe that's why offensive linemen have a distinct personality. If you were to talk with a bunch of football players, you'd probably be able to figure out which behemoths were the offensive linemen.

I've found that these workhorses of the game are usually great guys. Humble. Not too flashy. Hospitable. They take time to chat with fans.

On the field, they are hard-working, consistent, and team-oriented.They are the blue-collar men of football. They labor in the trenches where lesser men fear to tread.

Let me tell you about one such unit—a bunch of guys I'm sure you've never heard of.

It was my senior year at the University of Southern California, and the Trojans were picked to go absolutely nowhere. The pro scouts stayed away in droves.

Yet as a unit, we had one thing going for us. We knew that hard work, commitment, dedication, and sacrifice was all we had to rely on. That and each other. In the end, it was all we needed.

Picked to go nowhere, we ended up at the Rose Bowl on January 1, where we beat the Ohio State Buckeyes. And much of our victory hinged on the success of the offensive line. We were just a bunch of ordinary guys focused on a set of goals, determined to accomplish them in our ordinary way.

But the outcome was more than ordinary. It took a great effort to make the small differences that made all the difference in the world to our team.

Whenever I see that kind of effort from dads, I try to tell them they're making a difference in this world.

Dads have to keep reminding themselves that it's not the big stars of this world who'll bring a society back from the brink of destruction. It's men like you who are with your kids every day, quietly influencing them for now and for eternity.

Like an offensive lineman, you won't be receiving a lot of accolades, trophies, or recognition. It's not a glamorous job.

Like an offensive lineman, you'll butt heads with the opposition, get knocked down a few times, and have no recourse but to get up and go at it again.

And like an offensive lineman, sometimes you'll receive only what might look like penalties—loss of free time, sacrifice, commitment, and hard work.

But the rewards will come, and they're rewards that can't be measured in something as temporal as money.

So take the offensive lineman challenge. Give up yourself for the good of those kids God has entrusted to you. Be an unsung hero in the life of your children—and in the bigger picture—your country. Be a dad to the rescue!

Hey now, even superstars take first steps first.

DRIVE YOUR OWN CAR

As we discussed in the opening chapter, many people today feel as if they need a celebrity as a positive role model for their children. I'm amazed at how readily these folks are willing to hand over their kids' minds and hearts to someone else—a media-created illusion, no less.

This is like giving up the keys to your car and letting someone else drive your kids' lives. The danger is that the illusion you believe about the role-model driver may not be true. In fact, he or she may be driving your kids where you don't want them to go.

Imagine it this way: A role model is driving a passenger bus full of thousands of sports fans. He has the keys to your children's lives on his dash, along with all the other passengers. Sometimes the bus goes where you want it to go, sometimes it doesn't.

Eventually, your children's role model, the driver of the bus, crashes in the middle of nowhere and we all wake up to the reality that the driver was someone other than we expected—and he may not even have recognized that he had passengers aboard.

Obviously, illusions are not very responsible drivers.

When you drive your children, as long as you're following God's guidelines for living, you can have confidence that they're going safely in the right direction.

Sure, they may take little sidetrips on the Big Star Role Model Express, but their final destination is up to you. And guess what? It's you they want to pass the miles with anyway, Dad.

THEY'D RATHER RIDE WITH YOU

It's true. I'm not making this up to make you feel good. A poll published in Parade magazine bears it out. They reported on a survey first printed in *Careers and Colleges* magazine. The question asked was, "Whom do you admire?"

"More than seven out of ten teenagers chose their moms and dads over a group of celebrities. Among the female choices, 79 percent of teenagers picked their mothers. Oprah Winfrey was next with 10 percent, Hillary Rodham Clinton, 7 percent, and 3 percent chose Steffie Graff. Among the males, 73 percent of the teens picked their fathers, Denzel Washington was second with 12 percent, President Clinton got 8 percent, and 7 percent picked Charles Barkley."[1]

What a huge opportunity our kids' confidence provides us as we face the task of fathering!

One of the key players in the recent success of the San Francisco 49ers is tight end Brent Jones. His experiences with his dad show how a child's eagerness to be led and a dad's willingness to lead can work together.

"My dad influenced my life the most as I was growing up," Jones recalled, "because he would spend a lot of time with us. My mom was always there, too. But it was my dad who always said, 'Whenever you guys want to play ball, you let me know, and I'll always find time to play.'

"If we wanted to take batting practice for three hours or toss footballs or shoot hoops—he'd always spend time with us, no matter what. The older I get, the more I realize he had to sacrifice something for those times."

A little like an offensive lineman, don't you think? Giving. Sacrificing. Contributing.

And, of course, modeling. Notice that what Brent's dad did was nothing exotic, nothing expensive, nothing complicated. But he knew how important it was to "drive his own car."

For Karl Mecklenburg, growing up with father almost led him toward a profession in medicine—simply because of his dad's example. "My father is a physician. He's always loved his work, and I guess that's what made me want to become a doctor—until I found out how much I loved football.

"My dad's whole approach to life is something I've tried to emulate.

He's a very patient, loving man. He was dedicated not only to his work, but also to us.

"Being an obstetrician, he was on call often, and he'd come and go. But he was at almost all my football games. I know it was difficult for him to schedule, but it really meant a lot to me. I'm sure he had a lot of things he had to do, but he took the time and spent it with my sister and brothers and me."

If we are to come to the rescue of our children in a dangerous, confused world, we dads need to have that kind of dedication. Your kids really would rather ride with you. And if they do, they'll remember.

How can you let your kids know that you're as available for a spin as the latest TV rerun?

PREPARE TO DRIVE THE DISTANCE

When we're in the middle of raising a family, making a living, and coping with our own difficulties, it's easy to lose perspective. Are we making a long-range difference? Because we can't see the final destination, we wonder if we'll get anywhere before we run out of gas.

Perhaps the story of a famous Super Bowl incident can encourage you to look long-range—to trust that what you're teaching your children now will bear fruit many years ahead.

As you may recall, Don Beebe of the Buffalo Bills was involved in one of the most bizarre and humorous plays in Super Bowl history. It was Super Bowl XXVIII in Atlanta and the Bills were playing the Cowboys.

Late in the lopsided contest, which Dallas was winning by several touchdowns, Leon Lett of the "Boys" picked up a loose ball and took off toward the end zone uncontested. As he neared the goal line, out of nowhere came Beebe, running as fast as he could. Just before Lett could cross the line and enjoy the glory of a Super Bowl touchdown, Beebe stripped the ball out of his hands.

Here's Beebe's take on the incident. "A lot of people call Leon a lot of names for that. They thought he was showboating. People were telling me that they were so glad I knocked the ball out of that hotdog's hands. I see a different picture.

"I told them, 'Wait a minute. You have to put yourself in his position. He's a defensive lineman, he's never scored a touchdown, and here he's going to score a touchdown in the Super Bowl. So he got a little excited and just put the ball out there. It wasn't like he was dancing or going in backward. He just stuck the ball out there.'

"I didn't see any problem with that at all.

"Well, here comes this little pipsqueak down the sideline who knocks it out of his hands.

"It really wasn't that big of a deal with me, because I was basically doing my job. I was doing what I thought was right, and all I saw was the fumble. I saw a man pick it up from the opposing team, and my job then was to tackle the guy.

"The score was 52 to 17 at the time, so many people asked me, 'Why did you even run down the field?'

"It was no big deal. I was just doing my job.

"I firmly believe the reason I reacted that way was from the Christian upbringing that my mom and dad instilled in me. They helped me learn the right morals and values it takes to make it in this world. My father instilled in me a never-say-die, never-quit attitude. Give it a hundred percent every time you're out there."

None of those three fathers—Jones, Mecklenburg, nor Beebe—knew their sons would grow up to become role models on a national scale. They didn't know their influence would be seen in their boys' conduct on national television.

None of us knows how far-reaching the influence we have on our kids will be. Yet for those who invest their all, for those willing to stay on the longrange road—there's a way to drive the distance.

BLOWOUTS WILL OCCUR

Recently I spent a long day of travel in the car with my family. By dinner time, I was frazzled. On edge. Starving. We were all trying to figure out where to go eat. The girls were squabbling; each one wanted a different fast-food place. My wife was asking me questions (I can't remember what about now) at the same time as my son was badgering me to help him decide which team I thought he should pick to play against on his video game.

I blew an emotional tire. I lost it. Period. I'm too embarrassed to describe exactly what that looked like, but it wasn't attractive—or comfortable—or much of an example to my kids.

Immediately I thought of this book. And I realized once again how often it needs to be said: You will have bad days. You will blow it. You may be driving your own car—but there'll be moments when your family wishes you weren't! They'll wish they were in some other car. And you will too!

This is true with any job—not just fathering. We don't expect to be perfect at work, or even in our hobbies. So why not expect setbacks as dads?

Some days, you will crash, lose your way, or have a blowout. But the good news is this: it won't be irreparable.You'll probably squirm and maybe shout a little and then finally end up at McDonalds or Burger King —ready to start all over again.

CHOOSE YOUR SWORD

All right, guys. It's time to leave the car behind—and choose your weapon.

In their book *The Hidden Value of a Man,* authors Gary Smalley and John Trent wrote about two swords—silver and gold—that represent a father's work life and home life.

The silver-handled sword is the one we grew up with and learned to use through our early years of manhood. We've obtained it through sweat and grit and long hours of labor. It's the sword we use on the job. This sword is our constant sense of protection and an "equalizer in a rough and tumble world."

The second sword is the golden sword. Smalley and Trent described it as the one on display. It's been left there as long as we can remember—mounted over the fireplace, as it were. They called it "something you may hardly notice, something to dust twice a year.

"Most of the men you know in the workaday world want to wield the silver-handled sword."

Yet at home, the authors wrote, "The [silver] sword that looks so impressive in the marketplace seems a heavy, awkward thing when you walk through your front door in the evening. It can catch on the screen door, even knock over the umbrella stand and a vase or two."

The gold sword, the authors explained, points toward modeling. We use the gold sword at home with our wife and kids. "The gold sword is what a man is, for good or ill on his day off, in his blue jeans and stocking feet. It's who he is when no one else is looking."

Perhaps this analogy can help us as we sort out our responsibilities to our family. I'm the kind of guy who tends to put different times, schedules, people and tasks into different boxes. It's tough for me to be in more than one box at a time.

So I try to think of the swords analogy when I come home from work, and it helps me realize I have to leave the football sword at the field.

"When you get home, think of that as the beginning of your second job."

GARY SMALLEY
JOHN TRENT
THE HIDDEN VALUE OF A MAN

I had a friend who once told me this: When you get home, think of that as the beginning of your second job. Your wife and kids have been waiting all day for you to come home and be their husband and daddy.

It would be easy to come home after a rough day of physical and mental stress, lie on the couch, and surf the channels with the remote in hand. But no matter how my day went, my family deserves the interaction, feedback, and love that I alone can give them.

I glance up and see the golden sword. And I realize that I've still got a battle to fight.

THE DAD GAP

For many of us, a pep talk to take charge in our children's lives is all we need. Once the problem is presented to us and we see that we need to become more active, we're eager to meet the challenge. We want to be a superdad.

But in the lives of far too many children in our society, the problem is not that Dad needs a kick-start, it's that Dad is not even around. If we're serious about this society being changed through the role modeling of dads, then we must take a close look at the problem of absentee fathers.

Let's begin with an example from a player in the NFL, running back Derrick Moore. "I grew up in Albany, Georgia. In my youthful days, I didn't have role models and men in my life who could influence me positively or spend a lot of quality one-on-one time with me.

"My mother basically raised all of us, and she did such a great job of teaching us about integrity and living the kind of life we could model. Unfortunately, it didn't give us everything we needed. Mom was able to meet most of our needs, but there's always a missing part to a person's life when the father is not there."

Unfortunately, what Moore experienced is becoming more and more common. Our country is a nation of absent fathers. A look at the statistics is frightening.

- "Nearly one in four of all American children are born to unmarried women, and many more are born into marriages that ultimately end in divorce."[2]
- "In some 87 percent of single-parent families in the United States, that parent is the mother."[3]
- "Studies of young criminals have found that more than 70 percent of all juveniles in state reform institutions come from fatherless homes. Children from broken families are nearly twice as likely as those in two parent families to drop out of high school."[4]
- The most fearsome and one of the fastest growing crimes in America is random murder committed by young men ages fifteen to nineteen. Fatherless boys account for 72 percent of all adolescent murderers and 70 percent of long-term prison inmates.[5]
- According to the National Fatherhood Institute, "As a result of out of wedlock births, divorce, and premature death, 5.6 million children under the age of 15 are being raised without a dad in the house."[6]
- "Fully 71 percent of those surveyed by *US News & World Report* said that it is very important for every child to have his or her father living at home, and nearly 8 in 10 think both fathers and mothers should spend more time with their kids."[7]

•"Tonight about 40% of US children will go to sleep in homes in which their fathers do not live."[8]

Daniel Patrick Moynahan said, "Once something that you consider deviant becomes widespread, the way you handle it is to redefine deviance. And that's what we've done with fatherlessness. We basically said 'Since we have so many fatherless families, maybe we can get along without fathers.'"[9]

"A 1940's child could say: my father had to leave for a while to do something important. The 1990's child must say: 'my father left me permanently because he wanted to.'"

DAVID BLANKENHORN
USA WEEKEND

That's the situation in America. Our "getting along without fathers" is wreaking havoc with the moral, emotional, and spiritual underpinnings of our land. We're not talking here about a "Christian" opinion. This is not just a "church" issue that no one outside the walls of religion is talking about. This is a concern of secular psychologists, writers, and other thinkers.

"Fatherlessness is the most harmful demographic trend of this generation," says David Blankenhorn, writing in USA Weekend. "It is the leading cause of the decline in the wellbeing of children. It is also the engine driving our most urgent social problems from crime to adolescent pregnancy to domestic violence. Yet, despite its scale and social consequences, fatherlessness is frequently ignored or denied, especially within our elite discourse, it remains a problem with no name."[10]

What happens when dads leave their children to fend for themselves? It's not a pretty picture, according to a story in the *South Bend Tribune.* Here's how one writer sees it:

"Boys bereft of fathers frequently mature with low self-esteem. They turn to peers for validation and role models. They have difficulty controlling aggressive urges, absent an adult of their sex to show them how to handle dangerous emotions.

HALFTIME POINTERS

Work on Your Personal Dad Stats

➢ Be your own promoter. Have you told your kids about the time you hit a triple with the bases loaded in Little League? Made a hard choice that cost you something? The time you helped a stranded motorist? Haul out the trophies and stories. Your kids will love it—and learn.

➢ Become more visible, available—and fun—than the questionable influences in your kids' lives. Show up at your children's school for lunch. Host a mega-slumber party for no reason at your house. Added plus: you'll become a hero to your children's best friends—and that will put you way ahead with your own.

➢ Think you're "losing it"? Take a parent's time out. When Sheryl is feeling especially tense or exasperated, she takes several minutes alone to regain a more positive perspective.

"The inner city with its father substitutes, the gang, and misogynistic males who grow up exploiting and/or brutalizing women, they've never known a man committed to one in a loving relationship, is a horror show preview of a fatherless world.

"Girls suffer, too. Without a father in the home, adolescent girls recklessly hunger for the affection missing in their lives. Among white families, daughters raised by their mothers alone are 164 percent more likely to bear a child out of wedlock. Then there's the not so small matter of parental discipline. The average 15-year-old boy towers over his mother, not his father. For younger children, a masculine voice has authority that can make them jump. The old man is the heavy artillery rolled out as a last resort.

"Just watching dad go to work every day to support his family, seeing him treat his wife lovingly and respectfully provides a powerful example of masculine responsibility.

"If we want men to stay with their children and fulfill their obligations, we'd better be recognizing and extolling their special contribution to the family. Men have to feel needed. They need assignments, jobs reserved for them alone. Mister Mom doesn't fill the bill."[11]

Russell Maryland of the Dallas Cowboys grew up with both parents in the home and involved in his life. But he also knows the streets, and he knows what's happening to kids without dads.

"If your parents don't get involved with you, somebody else will. And that person who gets involved with children doesn't always have the right agenda in mind.

"I think a lot of times parents let their children go and fend for themselves. All too often, you'll find those kids ending up being influenced by people off the streets, and a lot of times those can be in the form of gangs and drug dealers.

"When children grow up, they need that attention that only parents can give. They need somebody to look up to. They need somebody to emulate. The best person to emulate, I would say, is either one of the parents. But I think the father plays a major role, especially with a young man.

"I think the most important thing for a society is to have a group of strong men to back it. A lot of times I've seen in my neighborhood that there's a lot of families being broken and a lot of kids being brought up without fathers in the home. The mother has to be a father and mother. It can work, but I think it makes the mom's job harder."

In the world Maryland describes, fatherlessness is deadly. "The GDs (gang disciples) take their aggressive young boys under their wings, buy them fancy leather coats, Air Jordan basketball sneakers, and gold bracelets, and teach them to count money and evade the police. They treat them to visits to skating rinks in winter and bus tours in summer. They buy presents at Christmas and pass them out to everyone. A favored child eight to ten years old might be provided with a beeper and given drugs to carry or sell. The message, police say, is 'you belong to us.'"[12]

SURROGATE SUPERSTARS

GDs shouldn't stand for Gang Disciples. It should stand for God's Disciples. Even if fathers abandon their children, there are good role models in our society who could be discipling these young men. In a dadless society, the call goes out for surrogate superstars—men who will step in and assume that missing role.

That's what happened in Derrick Moore's life. Despite his lack of a strong father in his life, he became a fine football player, a model citizen, and a strong follower of Jesus Christ.

"As I was growing up through high school and my freshman year in college," Moore explained, "God strategically placed me among specific people who began to mentor me, take me under their wings, and teach me about life. They taught me about integrity, character, high morals, and what it takes to live in the world.

"A couple of guys who really stand out to me are Reggie Johnson and Antoine Marsh. They're really strong believers. These two guys, in my freshman year, gave me a real foundation to stand on. That foundation was Christ, who had shaped those guys into what they were.

"Coming as I did from adversity and poverty and coming from a community that was absolutely devastating, I think God just took control of my life and influenced it through people. To this very day I'm grateful for those relationships which made Derrick Moore what he is."

Offensive lineman Steve Wisniewski of the Los Angeles Raiders has a similar story, again demonstrating the importance of assisting fatherless dads in our society.

"A turning point in my life was at Penn State," said Wisniewski. "My parents were divorced after thirty-one years of marriage, and I was the youngest of six kids. That happened during my sophomore to junior year in high school, and it really shook me up.

"My mom and I had to sell our home and move to the 'other side of the tracks' and live in a really little apartment.

"It was a tough time for me. I didn't get to see my father as much, probably because of his shame over the divorce. He didn't want to be around me, so that was even tougher to someone who grew up idolizing his father.

"That hurt quite a bit, but I grew that much closer to my mother. I realized that I was going to do my very best through role models such as my brother Leo, who played with Penn State and the Colts, and guys like Mike Munchek and Matt Millen, other Christian athletes.

"I saw by watching them that Christians were people who weren't weak, needing to lean on a crutch, but they were men of strength, men God was using. I saw the joy and peace in their lives, and that was something I wanted. So through meeting these different Christian athletes, I decided to put my trust in Christ."

THE DISTANT SOUND OF ABSENT DADS

When we talk about absentee fathers, we usually refer to dads who have left the home to live elsewhere. Yet we can't underestimate the damage done by dads who remain in the home—yet refuse to actively participate in their children's lives.

"We talk about deadbeat dads. But what about emotionally deadbeat dads?"

VICE PRESIDENT GORE

For reasons that some seem eager to justify, but can't explain logically, these dads avoid being the role model they should be. And in doing so, they become the role model they shouldn't be.

They're emotionally absent dads—without official leave.

It's a problem that even people at the highest levels of government are wrestling with. "We talk about deadbeat dads," Vice President Gore says, "and clearly the phrase implies fathers who are not providing financially for their children. But what about emotional deadbeat dads? What about dads that provide money but no time?"

Absentee dads, whether they're physically or emotionally out of the home, create huge problems, as we've seen. Our first goal, then, is to make sure we're not guilty of either.

For some, this would take a total lifestyle change—a change in which selfish pursuits and individual goals have to take a back seat. For others, it would take a healing of fractured relationships and a redirection of a current lifestyle.

Until we make the changes necessary to become powerful role models, our children experience pressure that is like facing a power play in hockey.

When you face a power play, it means one or more of your players is in the penalty box, and your team has to play one or two players down. When we're minus a parent—either in a single parent household or when a resident father is emotionally absent, we disadvantage our kids in a hostile culture.

No hockey team that has a choice would play a man down. In our families, let's make sure we play at full strength. Let's make sure our kids don't hear the distant sound of an absent dad.

DADS WHO STEP INTO THE GAP

We've talked a lot about the dad gap, absent dads, and dads who aren't available at home.

But clearly, step-dads play a key part in the role-model game. They aren't just substitute dads, they're men who've stepped up to fill a dangerous hole on the family front lines. They're men who've committed to love a child they didn't bring into the world, but want to parent just the same.

The difficulties are greater in step-parenting than regular parenting. And every suggestion outlined in this book will be a bit harder to pull off if you're a step-dad. But for the same reason, your successes will mean even more.

I'm not a step-father, but I know how hard step-parenting is because I had a step-mother. We went head to head over the smallest things all through my teen years, especially. We fought over every possible issue, including whether or not I could watch *Love Boat*.

It's almost funny to look back on it now, but it was painful at the time. Today I see that we weren't really fighting about what we thought. We were just using other issues to hide behind more painful ones.

Stop and ask yourself at home: What's beneath the surface here? What's the bigger picture? Is your step-son angry at you because his step-brother got a car, or is he worried that he's not as "real" of a son to you?

If you need help, ask your wife. Woman are good at seeing below the surface of things. Once you have a deeper understanding, you can tackle the real issues instead of spinning without progress around the same old conflicts.

Here's a different slant on the step-parent issue. A friend of mine told me the other day how she grew up with a step-father who did almost everything wrong. "There was almost no modeling going on," she said. "Just the opposite! He blew it left and right.

"But looking back," she added, "I respect him deeply. He married a woman with four kids and he stayed. He supported them, endured their rejection, and botched his way through."

Now a friend of hers is leaving his wife, after twenty years of marriage, to pursue another woman. But this guy has been an incredible Christian father and role model to his little girls all these years.

"How will it feel to his daughters to suddenly have all that pulled out from under them?" she asks.

> *"You will find the extent of a man's determination on the goal line."*
>
> VINCE LOMBARDI

She goes on to make a surprising contrast. "Just think. With this adulterous father, one great act of leaving will tarnish years of good modeling and loving. But with my step-dad, one great act of *staying* made up for years of errors and fumbles."

Not just step-dads, but all dads should keep this in mind. Your role as a father of any kind, though hard, is a priceless, precarious gift. It's a reminder to your kids that some things can be counted on—and a lot can be forgiven.

LAUNCHING A ROLE-MODEL RESCUE

Taking responsibility as a role model for your family isn't easy. There are times when we feel as if we want out. The added demands on our lives seem overwhelming. Accepting responsibility burdens us.

As we've seen, society is telling us that it's all right to shirk our responsibilities and take the easy way out when life gets too difficult:

- If you don't like the demands of marriage, get a divorce.

- If you don't like reality, drugs are an easy alternative.
- If your job is difficult, you can always quit.

As a people, we have become freedom-and rights-oriented. As fathers, the world tells us that it's our right and freedom to hand off our reponsibilities to someone else: mothers, teachers, coaches, day care, churches, or other family members.

In the Bible, though, the Lord never suggests that anyone but parents has the responsibility for their children. God wants fathers to be their own family's role model. He wants us dads to carry the ball.

God has placed the goal line within our reach. As fathers, we can drop back, pass the ball to someone else, and hope that our family doesn't get blindsided. Or we can step up, take the responsibility the Lord has entrusted to us, and score. We have the power.

"Football doesn't have anything to do with it. It's no big deal to my kids that I play football. In fact, my son is a Dallas fan."

REGGIE WHITE
GREEN BAY PACKERS

Chuck Lane, the public relations director for the Green Bay Packers during the 1950s, jotted down some quotes from Vince Lombardi, one of the greatest coaches in NFL history. Lane had intended to someday publish them, but never did.

One day, I ran across his notes, scribbled on an old yellowing sheet of paper. One of the entries read, "You will find the extent of a man's determination on the goal line." Another that struck me was, "The goal line is the moment of truth; there is no room for a timid person there."

Likewise, we might say that there is no room for timid dads. If we plan to come to the rescue of our kids, they need to see us as strong, willing role models for them—always interested in showing them the way despite any obstacles in our path.

Speaking of people who aren't timid, I can't think of many men more brave than Reggie White, the "Minister of Defense." Reggie has established himself as one of the greatest football players ever, yet listen to what he says:

"When we get to heaven, God isn't going to let us in because we played football or basketball. He's going to let us in because of what Jesus did for us. And we're going to have to account for the impact we had glorifying God and doing what He called us to do. The same stipulations that are on me to live a godly life are on someone who's not playing a professional sport. We're no different."

According to White, the same is true of how he raises his kids. "Football doesn't have anything to do with it. It's no big deal to my kids that I play football. In fact, my son is a Dallas fan."

Now that we're on the subject of the Dallas Cowboys, I am impressed with something Jay Novecek told me. "If you start out being the most important role model for your children," he said, "they want to continue to grow with that. Then, no matter what they hear, no matter if it's Michael Jordan speaking, the biggest and most important role model they have will still be you. When you interact with them at a young age and continue to grow with that, you'll always have a good relationship with them."

That, of course, is the ideal, and it's truly great advice. There's nothing worse than the parent of a fifteen-year-old who comes crying to a counselor or pastor, saying, "My kid is messed up and we can't communicate. What can I do?"

The chance of rescue at that late date is a lot less likely than if Novaceck's suggestions had been in force from the beginning. But it's never too late to start trying harder. It's never too late to attempt a role-model rescue.

Remember all those times when you were a kid who dreamed of growing up to be a hero? Perhaps your dream was to step to the plate with a full count in the bottom of the ninth with the bases loaded and blast one into the seats. Or maybe you were going back to throw that Super Bowl-winning touchdown pass in overtime.

We all saw ourselves as heroes as kids, and I think when we grow older, we forget those dreams. Wouldn't it be great to resurrect those dreams and visualize again how we can be heroes?

But now we're in a position to make our heroism a reality. We *can* be heroes and role models for our kids. Instead of a quick bat or a strong throwing arm, we need the courage to stand tall and firm for our children.

Still, we need to dream. We need a vision for the kind of role model we want to be. Helen Keller, though blind and deaf, pointed the way for many people with her inspiring life. "Is there anything worse than blindness?" said Miss Keller. "Oh yes, a person with sight and no vision."

If we want to be role models who can rescue our children from the complex deceptions that threaten them, we need to be the visionary leaders of the family.

No matter what our situation—whether we're separated, divorced, or at home—we need to remember the promises we made to our kids. Just as we vowed to love our wife forever, for better or worse—when we had kids, we made an unspoken promise to care for them no matter what.

It's time for dads to break the cycles of bad vows and unfulfilled love in our families. It's time to change the destiny of a generation.

And you can—with God's help. You can leave your kids a new and lasting legacy of hope and godliness that will endure through new generations. You can be a superdad to the rescue. And in the next chapter, you'll find out better how.

PERSONAL TIME-OUT

1. In what ways am I an unsung hero to my children?
What have I done for them in the past two weeks that would make them know how special they are to me?

2. How do I balance out the tension between "driving my own car" and helping my children know which athletic role models are okay for them to "ride with" on occasion?

3. Am I an absentee dad in any way? If I'm absent physically, is there any solution on the horizon? (Careful, this may call for radical action.) If I'm absent emotionally, how can I punch back into my job as my kids' role model?

4. Do my kids see me as a rescuer or a destroyer? How can I help my kids learn to make good choices in the midst of a culture that often seems out to get them?

RUETTGERS' REFLECTIONS:

Football truths that also work in real life

Every game, every week, is the biggest game of my life.

Hard work overcomes shortcomings.

It starts with vision. You can't block what you can't see.

DAD MAXIMS:

Herschel Walker's dad, a farmer, lived out these words in life:
"Be who you are. And be happy who you are."

William White's dad, a GM worker, loved to tell his son:
"There's no such thing as a failure, just a quitter.
You never fail at something until you quit."

PART TWO

Power Plays: Tackling Role-model Strategies

CHAPTER FOUR

The Daddy Sneak

My dad is my role model because he is hard-working and not a quitter. He has shown me how to work hard and achieve my goals.

—THIRTEEN-YEAR-OLD BOY

Don't you just love the playoffs?

Whether it's the NCAA tournament, the NBA or NFL playoffs, or the Major League Baseball Championship Series, I'd guess that most fans find this the best part of any sports season. Everything's on the line, and one play could make the difference between moving on or going home.

What part of the season you like best, of course, depends on your perspective. If it's the last game of the season and you're out of the playoff picture, your body feels like it's a hundred years old, the stadium is half full, the media is on your case, and the players and coaches are afraid for their jobs—then the off-season may be your pick.

One of my favorite times on the sports calendar is training camp. But believe me, it's not the practices, bruises, or time away from my family that excites me. It's the fact that when we report, we're bursting with anticipation. What happened the year before doesn't matter anymore. We're Super Bowl bound!

In addition to the excitement of chasing the ring, there are other bonuses. Getting back together again gives us a chance to see the growth in everyone's family. It's amazing how quickly children grow up.

Sometimes during the off-season players grow too, but they don't grow up. They grow out, gaining so much weight that it makes them ineffective as football players. Although most players come to camp well-conditioned, somewhere in the NFL you can usually find at least one player who's eating his way out of a job.

LAZY DADS DIE HARDER

During the first few days of camp, players spend a lot of time talking about what they've done since they were last together. It reminds me of the excitement of coming back to school in September and seeing all your buddies after summer vacation. The whole room is buzzing with talk and laughter.

But eventually we turn the conversation toward workouts. We grill each other with questions. What type of conditioning program have you used? What type of weight-lifting program did you follow? What about the nutrition and supplement program?

"We add yesterday's successes to today's lessons to create tomorrow's victory."

KEN RUETTGERS
GREEN BAY PACKERS

No matter how much bragging is done about workouts, the true tests of how well a player has prepared are the strength and conditioning tests. That's the moment of truth. How well did we follow the laws of nature God set up at creation?

You can't break those laws without being discovered. Hard work pays off. Hard work shows. So does no work—on the field or at home. Have you stepped on a scale lately, Dad?

Football, like fathering, would be easy if we were all great athletes—no effort required. But God's plan for our bodies doesn't work that way. And I, for one, am glad. Hard work helps us overcome our weaknesses. And it reveals our efforts at consistency, sacrifice, and commitment.

What if it were easy to lose weight and build up your body like Arnold Schwarzenegger? There would be no premium in looking so good. Everyone would be a lean, mean weight-lifting machine. That's the beauty of God's free-will system. It incorporates natural consequences with our choices—and you can't cheat. But strength and conditioning are only part of what's needed if you want to be a good, solid performer—or father.

To be a complete player, study the game tapes, pour over the play book, use the proper techniques, get the proper rest, maintain your focus on the team's goal, keep your emotions in check, and work hard in practice.

At home this translates to: Know your family and how to best love each member. Get rest! Take care of yourself so you're in good shape to help score at home. Keep your emotions in check. And be understanding of the feelings of others.

Just as in football, it would be nice if fathering were easy. If we could just wake up one morning knowing all we needed to know and doing everything we needed to do. We'd all be the world's greatest dads.

But it's not going to happen that way. In fact, being a good father is even more difficult than being a great athlete. Just like my friends in training camp, we can sit around talking about what good fathers we're becoming.

But actions speak louder than words. We can't cheat the system. If we don't put out the effort, we may appear to get by. It may seem like we are doing an adequate job, but game day is coming.

The moment of truth for a father is when our children are faced with difficult decisions or temptations. It's too late then to play catch up. If we haven't poured our influence into our children little by little, precept by precept, we aren't going to like what the game tapes tell us.

That's why for dads, in a sense, it is always training camp. And the strategies that work the best are slow and steady, but sure. I call this the "Daddy Sneak." It's an approach that may only look like a lot of practice on the surface—but it all adds up to a great power play.

REAL MEN PRACTICE

Did you ever notice that sports training camps don't last just one day? We can't arrive at camp on Saturday morning, work out a couple of times, have a meeting, and then go out and play the Minnesota Vikings the next day.

We'd be out of shape, disorganized, and embarrassed.

Instead, we build one exercise on another, one scheme on another, one drill on another—until we're prepared for the war that happens each game in the NFL.

Football is unusual because we get together to practice far more than we get together to play games. During a week, we may hit the practice field five or six times and play just one game. In most other sports, such as baseball, there are more games than practice.

I think being a good dad is more like football. We practice and practice — for the infrequent game. As dads, you too will practice and practice so that when crucial times come in your children's lives, you'll respond with strength.

Someone once told me that one of the credos Miami Dolphin coach Don Shula lives by is this: "When things aren't going well, work harder. When things are going well, work harder."

"When things aren't going well, work harder. When things are going well, work harder."

DON SHULA
MIAMI DOLPHIN COACH

I remember watching Herschell Walker when he first blasted his way on the sports scene as a sensational running back for the University of Georgia. His football exploits were astounding, but his body was just as amazing. He was incredibly strong, and people wanted to know how he got that way.

I found the answer when I talked to Herschell about role models.

"I worked hard all my life," he explained. "I baled hay, picked peas, picked cotton. What was big in my family life was the responsibility of getting it done. I watched my parents go to work day after day and never complain. They raised seven kids without complaining about what they had to do.

"My father was the only boy among seven children, and his father was killed when my father was twelve. My dad went to work on a farm to help his sisters and mother. I think that's an inspiration in my life. You have so many people complaining today, and yet we have a lot if we're willing to work at it. We have too many people today who are too lazy to go out and work at anything.

"I don't ever remember my dad quitting. He used to work on cars—

but not because it was a hobby. When you have seven kids, you just don't take the car to a shop. You're going to fix it yourself. Or if something broke in the house, dad would be there two or three days putting it all together, not quitting until it worked. He just never quit."

That's the attitude we need as dads.

And that's the attitude of real men.

In America we've too often detached masculinity from the roles of husband and father, encouraging men to be irresponsible, violent, predatory. Real men don't prove their masculinity through violence, sexual exploits, or amassing large fortunes. Real men are committed fathers and loving husbands.

Fathering is always a learning process. No dad starts out knowing it all with the arrival of his first-born—or even his second or third. Parenting is ever changing, so we must be ever learning.

That means practice, and that calls for a lot of contact with our kids.

FATHERING AS A CONTACT SPORT

When I was at USC, head coach John Robinson and his staff wanted us to understand that if you work at improving little by little, it adds up to a lot. A lot of work makes a little bit of difference every day, they would tell us, which adds up to something that could make the difference in the game.

I was an offensive lineman at USC, and we had a strong running game. Our whole objective was to wear our opponents down in the first three quarters so by the fourth quarter we'd win the game. We'd chip away little by little, until we were dominating our opponent.

In some ways, we dads can apply the one-step-at-a-time approach to influence our children. But to do so, we have to be engaged with them, face to face, run for run. We have to participate in their victories and in their defeats. We can't just be distant observers. We need to make fathering a contact sport.

Because we live in an interactive world, we should try to be part of our children's world as interactive fathers—if we ever want to compete for their attention and respect. If we don't, we'll miss an opportunity that can't be fully recovered.

So what are the one-at-a-time steps to success? How do we dads block out, wear down, and sneak up on the competition? Here are three ways:

DOMINATE THE CLOCK

One study has revealed that the average five year old spends only twenty-five minutes a week in close interaction with his father. Yet, the same child spends twenty-five hours a week watching television.[1] The average preschooler watches more television in three years than the average college student spends in the classroom in four years.

If the above statistic of twenty-five minutes a week of dad-child interaction is consistent through a child's first eighteen years, the sad result is that the two of them will spend less than four hundred hours together before the son or daughter becomes an adult.

"The average teenager will listen to and watch 11,000 hours of rock music and rock videos. More than twice the time they will spend in class."

AMERICAN ACADEMY OF PEDIATRICS

According to the American Academy of Pediatrics, there's another statistic to mix into the equation. "Studies show that between 7th and 12th grades, the average teenager will listen to and watch 11,000 hours of rock music and rock videos. More than twice the time they will spend in the class."[2]

Is it any wonder that people like Madonna, Ice T, Marky Mark, and Snoop Dog E. Dog are having a bigger impact on our children than we are?

If contact parenting is our goal, and if influencing our children little by little until they're mature is our objective—we need some help. Let's see what the Bible has to say.

Thousands and thousands of years before we ever thought of the term interactive, Moses suggested that kind of parenting. Notice the ongoing, constant interaction that is suggested by his words in Deuteronomy 6:

"These commandments that I give you today are to be upon your hearts. Impress them on your children. Talk about them when you sit at home and when you walk along the road, when you lie down and when you get up. Tie them as symbols on your hands and bind them on your foreheads. Write them on the doorframes of your houses and on your gates" (vv. 6-9).

That sounds like more than twenty-five minutes a week. It sounds more like a continual effort, carried out amid the mundane tasks of life.

It's not about taking our kids to church and hoping the folks there teach them well. It's not about sending them to a good Christian school, either. These things may be a part of the plan, but the main responsibility lies with us parents.

Time means contact. Time means interaction.

Time may even mean play.

One thing I really enjoying doing with Matthew is playing catch with him. We try to do it almost every day when I'm not out of town or too banged up. Sometimes it turns into a neighborhood contest with other kids from the block.

But often it gives us quality time to spend alone together, one on one. As we toss, we talk. It's a time to ask him questions, find out what he's thinking, how he's feeling, how school went, how his friends are doing. It's a way to get to know him a little bit better every day.

It also gives me an opportunity to encourage Matthew. I can give him positive feedback in regard to his life—and how he's catching and throwing the ball. I get to say, "Hey, that's a great throw, Matthew, great job!" Or, "I think you're a great brother, Matthew."

The activity might be different for you—building models, doing chores, playing on the computer, working in the shop, or collecting stamps together. It can be almost anything. That quality one-on-one time is a legacy we leave our kids—and enjoy ourselves, too.

TAKE YOUR GAINS WITH PATIENCE

In a weight room where I often worked out, there was a leg press machine that I used to build up my leg strength.

It was a big machine, and it looked immovable. Maybe that's why it wasn't bolted to the floor.

HALFTIME POINTERS

Big-Picture Home Investments

➢ Post a Family Creed on your refrigerator. Ours, borrowed from Mike Singletary's book, *Singletary on Singletary*, goes as follows:

- Love God and Jesus.
- Love one another.
- Always obey Mom and Dad
- Always pray for one another.
- Put family before friends.

➢ Create a Family Constitution. We post ours next to the Family Creed. The Family Constitution lists basic rules and consequences. Draw it up together at a family meeting. Your kids will be more willing to obey rules that they have helped make.

➢ Look for long-term projects to do together. They're great for letting you show love and commitment over time. Ideas: an impossibly complex jig-saw puzzle, an on-going coin or baseball collection, a restoration project, learning a new sport together, or reading a book series.

Yet as time passed and as my fellow weight-lifters and I struggled, strained, and pushed, this leg press machine loaded with heavy weights imperceptibly "walked" inch by inch across the room.

We'd notice the progress of the machine only after time had passed and because we could measure its movement in relationship to other objects in the weight room.

Sometimes that's how our influence affects our children. If we try today to see how they've grown compared to yesterday, we can't see any change. But over the course of time, we see the slow, steady movement toward maturity.

Think of the first time you took your child outside to throw a ball around with him or her. You threw, the child missed, and someone picked up the ball. It was frustrating. You wanted to say, "Look. Here's how you throw and catch," and the child would say, "Oh, I see. Like this?" And that would've been the end of it.

It doesn't happen that way. It's throw, pick up. Throw, pick up. And on it goes.

In life it is tell, pick up. Tell, pick up. We cannot expect our children to immediately learn the great moral concepts of life that are so important. They take time and patience.

A couple years ago, we purchased a Suburban to haul around our growing family. But before we could drive it, we had to wait to receive the license plates in the mail. I remember how excited I was when they arrived.

What was really exciting, though, was to have the help of my son as we put the license plate on. Together, we took the screws out and inserted the screws to hold the new plate. With his help, it probably took about fifteen minutes longer than it should have.

But the real joy of this event wasn't that it signified a new car, but that it signified a job well done—and done together. A little job became a father and son task. His eyes lit up when we stood back and looked at the license plate he'd helped his dad put on the car.

GUARD YOUR POSITION

Many mornings as I shave, my son watches every stroke. Knowing that he's watching me, I look back into the mirror to make sure I don't cut myself. Yet I see the larger picture, that in everything I do I'm modeling for my son.

Our kids are watching us intently. Sometimes we notice, sometimes we don't. But they're always watching our show, taking mental notes. And those notes go far beyond how we shave and comb our hair. They're watching how we live.

I remember one weekday afternoon after returning from an intense workout. I was exhausted, so I lay down on the couch to shut my eyes and take a snooze.

My son was about three years old at the time, and we had just returned from Green Bay. It was a beautiful California spring day. I awoke to the sound of the lawn mower. The man we hire to cut the grass was mowing the backyard.

When I sat up from the couch, I looked into the backyard and there was my son, pushing his toy bubble-making lawn mower behind the gardener. *Whoa, wait a minute!* I thought. I got that lawn mower so I could mow the yard with *my* son and he could follow me around.

But there went Matthew, mowing right behind the gardener, following the man's tracks in the lawn.

I want my son to follow my tracks. Not someone else's.

Are you ready to risk being so closely watched and imitated?

If we catch ourselves sleeping while our kids are looking for role models, we'll lose out on some important contact opportunities. What's more, the substitute who fills our vacant position may not be as benign as our gardener.

Art often imitates life, which I think happens in *The Lion King*. This Disney cartoon feature presents a good example of how a father can influence his son and how a son can pick up bad advice from others.

Simba is the son. His father, Mufasa, is the king. As he teaches Simba the rules and protocol of his position, he explains that a king can do whatever he wants, but there's more to it than getting your way all the time.

At one point when young Simba is being disciplined, his father calls him. As Simba walks up, he steps into a hole. But what he really stepped into was his father's footprint. He suddenly realizes that he's not even close to filling his father's footsteps.

Mufasa was preparing his son through his teaching to follow him one day to the throne. However, because of the interference of Mufasa's evil brother, Scar, the line of succession must wait.

Mufasa is killed, and Simba runs away, thinking he's responsible.

Simba is eventually rescued by a warthog named Pumba and a rodent-type animal named Timone. They teach him a new model: When the world turns its back on you, you turn your back on it. They also teach him "Hacuna Matana," which means no worries for the rest of your days. It's a problem-free philosophy.

Young Simba adopts the philosophy. He has forgotten the good things his father taught him, and he no longer feels like the heir to the throne.

Only when another animal convinces him to return to his homeland

and claim what his father promised him does Simba succeed.

Mufasa couldn't guard his position with his son after he died. Evil influences such as Scar's—or even questionable influences, such as the warthog's—had free reign to interfere. Yet it's important to note that Mufasa's legacy survived within Simba.

As fathers, you strive to be sure your children understand the right way to live. You want to leave a big footprint, too. But you also know that someday your kids will go out on their own like Simba and be influenced by all kinds of philosophies.

The prospect can feel threatening.

But here's the good news. If you guard your position, your own loving example of the right way to live will make an indelible impact on your kids. And with God's help, they will never turn away from it—no matter how many Scars they face.

PERSONAL TIME-OUT

1. Would I prefer throwing a long bomb to employing the steady, slow "Daddy Sneak"? What is most frustrating to me about the contact approach to role modeling?

2. In sports, did I teach the principle of practice when I began to teach my children to throw and catch? What other concepts take them a long time to grasp and make their own?

3. What have I done in the past week that I could call close contact parenting? How long did I spend with my children?

4. What other lessons from *The Lion King* can I, as a dad (Mufasa), glean as I talk with my child (Simba)?

RUETTGERS' REFLECTIONS

Football truths that also work in real life

One play at a time, one game at a time.

You win the battle on the first step.

Nothing great comes easy.

CHAPTER FIVE

The Triple Threat

My role model is my grandpa because he quit school after eighth grade yet he's one of the smartest people I know.

—JUNIOR HIGH STUDENT

As an offensive lineman, I've grown to appreciate the skills of the guys behind me that I'm trying to protect. The key man behind the line, of course, is the quarterback. We've been blessed in the past few years with a good one in Bret Favre.

As quarterbacks settle into their patterns as signal-callers, some like to stay in the pocket and fire away, specializing in their passing game. This kind of QB wants his line to hold off the rush a little longer. Otherwise, he's a sitting duck back there.

Other quarterbacks like to scramble behind the line of scrimmage. They have about as much interest in staying in the pocket as a cat has in staying in a tub of water. If they have to, they'll go from sideline to sideline in search of that elusive open receiver. It's a chore to block for a guy like that because you never know where he's going to be.

A third type of signal-caller likes to run the ball. Sure, he has to know how to pass and hand off, but a running quarterback seems to have a Barry Sanders gene in him. He gets his kicks from rushing through the line toward a first down.

Imagine what would happen if you had all three of those guys wrapped up in one quarterback. A guy who can stand and throw, who can throw on the go, and who can pick up a first down on his own. That kind of triple-threat quarterback would be hard to stop. And believe me, a bit hard to block for.

But then, no one ever asks offensive linemen what they prefer. We just do our jobs.

Like the job of being a quarterback, the job of being a role model has a triple-threat possibility, too. It's one of our biggest power plays possible.

We normally think of role models as people who are somewhat one-dimensional in scope. I'd like to suggest that we scrap that idea and see the possibilities that exist in modeling on a greater spectrum.

As we've already observed, our society needs a higher level of commitment from its leaders—in the sports world, the entertainment media, the political arena, the workforce, and the home. That commitment calls for willing, ready people, along with a new vision of how we can guide our nation's children.

I'm talking about "triple-threat role models." These people demonstrate moral, godly behavior in three life arenas: their home and family, their daily communities, and society at large, including people they don't know.

Have you ever looked at the life of our Lord Jesus Christ to see how he modeled his exemplary life? Notice that there are three levels. On the first level, Jesus lived perfectly before His family—Joseph and Mary and his brothers and sisters.

His level two relationships included close ties with a group of men and women He had regular contact with, including a group of twelve men who He called disciples.

And finally, in what we might call the level three situation, Jesus influenced thousands of people who knew Him only by reputation, by having an infrequent audience with Him, or by what others told them about Him.

But there's an unusual and exciting twist with Christ. We've been affected by Jesus on the third level in such a way that we can also relate to Him intimately on the first level.

Obviously, the apostolic age ended with the deaths of those who knew Jesus personally. But the third level of influence has continued on to this day, making a bridge to the first level through teachings from

Scripture about Jesus' life, death, and resurrection.

Look at John 20:29, where Jesus says, "Blessed are those who have not seen and yet have believed." If we've accepted Jesus Christ as Savior, we're those blessed people. As we first read and hear about Jesus, He affects us in a long-distance way, but the relationship turns intimate and first level once we become His follower.

Not only did Jesus model the three levels of influence, but He also taught us to do the same. What else could we conclude from Acts 1:8, which says, "You will be my witnesses in Jerusalem [level 1], and in all Judea [level 2] and Samaria, and to the ends of the earth" [level 3]?

With that biblical pattern in mind, let's look a little closer at the way we can each be a triple-threat role model.

LEVEL ONE: The first level includes our responsibility as the parents of our children. We should concentrate on them, because we're the key to their success in this life.

LEVEL TWO: The second level of role modeling within our circle of influence relates to folks with whom we have regular contact—our extended families, our co-workers, our neighbors, and our friends.

LEVEL THREE: The third level moves beyond the group we see every day and out into the world. It includes people that we may have only infrequent contact with. For example, the long-distance influence I might have on kids who look up to me as an athlete but who will never meet me.

Or the effect I will have on you as you read this book. Well-known Christian writer Philip Yancey, who's written such popular books as *Where Is God When It Hurts* and *Fearfully and Wonderfully Made* understands his role as a third-level role model. "Most of the people I've affected," he muses, "I've never met."

Clearly, when we begin to pursue the many avenues of influence we have in our everyday lives, we see how important modeling is. And clearly our nation would be changed if each person would employ the triple threat for the power of good.

LEVEL ONE MODELING: FACE TO FACE ON THE FAMILY FRONT

As a football player, it's easy for me to look good to people. On a football card I appear glossy and smooth, and on the back I sound good, too. On TV, I look like a football player is supposed to look—we have great-looking uniforms at Green Bay. I go out on speaking engagements dressed up in my tie and coat, armed with my notes, and appear to be a pretty spiffy guy.

All of that is relatively easy. What's hard is to live my life in a way that makes me look good at home. My wife and kids see me just as I am — close up. They know when I'm grumpy. They know what makes me upset. Matthew, Katherine, and Susan even know how I treat their mom.

Believe me, level one modeling is perhaps the toughest task we have. There can be no fakery, no pretense, no cover-up.

We are who we *really* are at home. We can't and should never forget that eager, impressionable eyes are watching. I tend to agree with the old Chinese proverb that says, "It is harder to lead a family than to rule a nation."

> *"Your success as a family, our success as a society, depends not on what happens in the White House, but what happens in your house."*
>
> FORMER FIRST LADY BARBARA BUSH

Former First Lady Barbara Bush knows something about both. During her husband George's four years in the White House, Mrs. Bush endeared herself to many Americans for her strong emphasis on the family. Notice the wisdom in these words to a group of professionals: "As important as your obligations as a doctor, a lawyer, a business leader will be, you are a human being first, and those human connections with spouses, with children, with friends are the most important investment you will ever make.

"At the end of your life, you will never regret not having passed one more test, winning one more verdict, or not closing one more deal. You will regret time not spent with a husband, a child, a friend, or a parent.

"Whatever the era, whatever the times, one thing will never change:

Fathers and mothers, if you have children, they must come first. Your success as a family, our success as a society, depends not on what happens in the White House, but what happens in your house."

What happens in the house doesn't always revolve around dad, because he often has to be out of the house for his job. But the key consideration that we have to consider is this: What happens when Dad does come home? Is his presence a boon or a hindrance?

To put it bluntly—are we being the kind of role model for our kids that will help them grow to be functioning, godly citizens in the next century?

I was talking with Michael Samply, a friend who is a Christian psychologist in Bakersfield, California. "After being at work all day," he said, "you come home and you start the most important job of the day. Being a husband and a father."

That made me think. I've spent all day pushing around defenders, running sprints, studying plays, lifting weights, and giving one hundred percent of my physical, mental, and emotional energies and skills to help the team get better. By the time the coaching staff lets us go, I'm running pretty much on empty.

You may have been balancing a ledger, selling clothes, fixing computers, pumping gas, or putting wheel covers on cars. It doesn't matter. You're just as whipped as I am when you finally drag yourself home.

It would be easy, in that situation, to put it on cruise control for the rest of the evening and coast till the eleven o'clock news.

That, however, would be putting things backward. If Samply is right and my most important job lies ahead when I pull the car into the garage, then I need to give my family the same effort I just gave the Packers.

That's the intriguing part of his statement. What would happen if we were to put one hundred percent of our energies into role modeling and being a dad, just as we do at work? If we worked at home as if we were going to get a quarterly review of our performance?

Imagine the impact we would make if the kids knew that when Dad came home, he would be completely theirs to enjoy!

That's the kind of work ethic it takes to make a difference in level one role modeling. And that's what it takes to unleash the power God's given us to be great fathers. This is a calling within our reach. We can do this.

I only hope I can be half the parent for Matthew that the biblical Daniel's folks must have been for him. Daniel was a young man of integrity. As a teenager standing before the king in a foreign land, he had the bravery to stick by his beliefs and what he knew God wanted him to do.

I sometimes wonder what Daniel's parents did right to bring up a young man of such integrity. Although there aren't a whole lot of hints about his parents, we can surely have as our goal that we want our kids to dare to be Daniels—and we want to be such parents.

"People who didn't know me loved me, and the people who knew me didn't love me."

KARL MECKLENBURG
DENVER BRONCOS

Karl Mecklenburg of the Denver Broncos told me that, at one time, he was guilty of violating the principle we're discussing. To be sure, he's changed his tune and ways—but I think his previous experience is valuable to explore.

Sadly, I think his story is not all that rare. In fact, I have to admit that early on in my own marriage, my style was very similar to the one Karl described.

"I thought it was my wife's job to take care of the kids, and I would take care of bringing the money home," he says. "I was very distant from my family. I wasn't really a part of it. I just wasn't all that involved.

"But then the Lord changed me. He opened up my eyes to what was important and what wasn't.

"When I had sixty-thousand people in the stands cheering for me, loving me, and caring about me, they had no idea who I was. I'd come home, and I was a stranger to my family. I guess my perspective was way out of whack. People who didn't know me loved me, and the people who knew me didn't love me.

"I didn't even realize what was happening until I needed my family during a time of crisis. I reached out to them and realized how much I needed them. What we dads have to do is take a look at ourselves, at our family, and see where we are. It's easy to go on day by day just living, try-

HALFTIME POINTERS

Three Ways to Change Your World

➢ Pick a "project" person. Focus on someone you believe in, and privately decide to invest extra time, energy, and love into his or her life for one year. Have coffee, call on the phone to talk. This idea is inspired by my friend John Anderson, who reached out to me the same way once.

➢ Volunteer with a friend. Choose a worthy cause or organization; bring a friend along. Volunteer work is a great way to bond with others, build friendships, and learn about yourself and life.

➢ Actively mentor your own children. Pick a problem area: a messy room, bad grades, or difficulty making friends. Talk through a simple plan for tackling the issue together, but most of all, let your children know you care.

ing to earn a living, and trying to do what seems important at the time. But in the long run you discover that it isn't nearly as important as what you've got at home."

The kind of level one modeling Karl is referring to has become increasingly complicated, and if the trend continues, it will become more so. It can seem overwhelming, can't it? When we start to panic, perhaps that's a good time to think about involving someone else in the process of modeling.

Family expert Gary Smalley has suggested, and I think rightly so, that parents of younger children may want to involve an adult friend as a supplementary role model. This allows the children to interact with an adult who is perceived differently from "their dad" or "their parents."

One example he offered was a friend of his who became a pen pal for his daughter. This friend encouraged her with his letters and attempted to help her be accountable.

This would be a great idea to incorporate with another family who has kids the same age as yours. You could be supplementary role models for each other's kids.

Smalley's idea is also a perfect lead-in for a discussion of the second level of role modeling. Level two involvement can radiate into so many facets of life. Let's see how it works and how it has touched lives for the better.

LEVEL TWO MODELING: TOE TO TOE WITH THOSE YOU KNOW

Perhaps the best way to begin thinking about the impact we can have at the level two stage of role modeling is to think of some situations where this kind of person has entered our lives and changed them for the better.

I can think of no better example than my friend and former teammate, Tunch Ilkin. As a professional football player, I'm blessed to have many friends and acquaintances. Sometimes I think I have more friends than any man deserves.

But only rarely in a man's life does an opportunity for a deep friendship make itself available—the kind that reminds a man who he is and what he stands for. A friendship based on something deeper than the commonality of a job, neighborhood, or political beliefs.

In the spring of 1993, the Green Bay Packers signed a tackle named Tunch Ilkin as a free agent. I was personally interested in this signing because I also earn my living playing offensive tackle for the Packers.

In fact, as the Packers' Transitional Designee that spring, I was expected to withhold my services throughout training camp over a contract dispute. To put it bluntly, I was expected to be a holdout.

When we signed Tunch, I recalled an incident from a previous football season. A newspaper reporter had asked me whether I deserved to go to the Pro Bowl.

I replied, "Look, I don't know who the guy is, but there's a Pittsburgh Steeler who went the whole season without giving up a single sack, and he didn't get voted in. If he didn't make it, I surely don't deserve to."

I later found out that the Steeler I was referring to was Tunch Ilkin, or as some people called him, Tuncher the Puncher. I remembered seeing

Tunch on game films, punching the daylights out of defensive ends around the league. What a competitor! He destroyed guys!

During a spring mini-camp after he'd signed, Tunch and I met. We had dinner together, discussed our faith, and swapped stories about our families. I told Tunch about the great accountability group I was part of back home in Bakersfield, California. We decided to start such a group in Green Bay during the season and add another lineman, Rich Moran.

When the pre-season got underway, I stayed home without a contract. I called Rich to find out what was going on in training camp, and he told me that Tunch had been moved to my position and that an article about him had appeared in the paper.

The article explained that Tunch was born in Turkey and that his father brought his family to America to find a better life for his wife and only child. In America the Ilkins lived in a one-room apartment, and Tunch had to sleep on a cot in the kitchen. It was a meager existence for a new immigrant family in America.

The story continued. After playing for Indiana, Tunch had been signed as a free agent by the Steelers and was cut his first year. Later, he'd been brought back, barely making the team. With the Steelers he earned All-Pro honors, was the team's captain, and was a two-time Pro Bowl selection. What a success story!

Here I was—holding out for more money, and a former immigrant from Turkey was taking my place. To say the least, I wasn't a very popular guy around the Green Bay area at that time.

Finally, after the last pre-season game—one week before the opener, I signed a new, four-year contract.

Before long, I was in the team hotel, and it was the night before our first game. My roommate from the year before had been cut during training camp, but I was pleasantly surprised to see that my new roomy was Tunch.

Later that night, after our team meetings and a snack, we were getting ready to hit the sack. I said, "Ya know, Tunch, even though I've been starting for eight years and feel honored to be doing so tomorrow, I feel unworthy to start in front of such a great player as you."

Tunch sighed deeply. "Well, Rut, I have played thirteen wonderful years in this league, and my role on this team is to be a back-up to you and Tootie (the other tackle). I'm sure you'll have a great game tomorrow. Remember to use the punch we've been working on all week."

Despite Tunch's words, I knew it bothered him—going from fan-favorite and team captain of the Pittsburgh Steelers in Pittsburgh to back-up in Green Bay where the fans didn't even know him. It would bother anyone.

I would later find out that it was indeed a difficult role for Tunch to accept. How could it not be—after all, he's human. It was something he prayed about throughout the season.

Most players in a similar position might feel angry, jealous, spiteful, cheated, and wronged—just for starters. Some players would want to take it out on the coaches and undermine the player starting in front of them at the expense of the team.

Not Tunch Ilkin. In fact, just the opposite was true.

Within the first week he'd become my close friend and mentor. He worked with me and other linemen during and after practice refining our technique. Although he was not starting, he was still a leader. He was still willing to give up himself for the benefit of others and the team, knowing that he was sacrificing his edge as an older yet wiser professional.

Many of today's generation of football players would call Tunch's behavior stupid. Not too long ago most people would have called it a virtue—a characteristic of sacrifice and leadership. Tunch was a true champion and role model—and his new teammates respected him because of it.

One of the techniques he helped me refine was the punch. It had always been a weakness in my game. In football, when an offensive lineman is pass blocking and focused on protecting the quarterback, one of the most effective weapons is the punch.

A good puncher, using both hands, explodes his fists—firing every muscle in his arms and back in a controlled violence. He plants them through the chest of the pass rusher, stopping his charge. The punch is what separates the men from the boys. It's the difference between a good block and a great block.

That's what Tunch brought back to my game. Every week the film would reveal the improvement of my punching technique. Every week we would get together after practice and work extra on it. We'd even talk about it over breakfast.

Breakfast was also a good time to enjoy some fellowship. Besides football and technique, we enjoyed talking about politics, values, and morals of society. We discussed tough decisions in life. We told stories of great victories and painful defeats, of embarrassing moments and of moments of conquest. We also talked about biblical heroes and the good and bad characteristics of each.

Our families enjoyed meals together, and our children played with each other. Together we attended Bible study and couples study and enjoyed our newly formed accountability group where Tunch, Rich, and I discussed many important issues in our lives.

Tunch and I formed a deep trust and bond in friendship. There were no secrets, and there was no need for either one of us to rely on a guarded position. Our shields were down. We were both committed to a friendship that goes deeper than the common denominators of job, community, or political beliefs.

Then the unthinkable happened.

The day after our eighth game, I came into the locker room, and Tunch was cleaning out his locker. He looked up at me and said, "They just cut me, Rut."

I was stunned. My friend Tunch had just been fired. My heart sank. I got a big lump in my throat and had to leave the locker room to regain my composure. The friendship that in just eight weeks had grown stronger than any other I'd ever experienced had just been cut short by the casualties of football.

My strong emotions surprised me. After eight years of football, I'd seen friends come and go, get cut, or retire due to sudden injury. But I had never felt this way.

I tried to rationalize Tunch's departure. After all, it was part of the game. It was to be expected. That's football. This wasn't supposed to happen. Not like this. Not in the middle of the season. Not in the middle of a great friendship. How could anything or anyone interrupt something so special!

I'm thankful that the following Sunday was a bye, and we didn't have a game for two weeks. I don't think I could have prepared myself in time to compete at the necessary level.

I could barely make it through a meeting that week. It was hard to watch films through teared-up eyes. Practice became torturous. I lost my desire to be part of such a pitiful occupation.

Dinners at home were just as tough. I lost my appetite because I'd lost my companion, mentor, and friend. My partner was leaving. I felt alone in battle. Isolated.

Finally I was able to find solace, but only through Tunch's explaining to me that he was content. He said he was content in his long and blessed career and in his desire to try to understand and follow God's new plan for his life.

I asked Tunch how I could feel so strongly about his being fired when I was part of a game that regularly found players prematurely departing for various reasons. After all, we had been close friends for only eight weeks.

He explained that it was because of our strong friendship. A friendship based in the Lord Jesus. There is no friendship stronger than one based in Him. Because the Holy Spirit was working in both our lives and our friendship, we were able to lay it on the line.

We didn't hold back when it came to sharing thoughts, beliefs, and emotions with each other. We put our arms out to each other knowing that they might get swatted down and used against us. We were willing to take a chance, to risk.

Lest I leave you with a negative feeling about this story, I'll end with some good news. Tunch was asked to come back to the team five weeks later, and he accepted the offer. We continued our friendship. And we went to the playoffs for the first time in twenty years as an organization.

During the off-season following Tunch's time in Green Bay, one of the coaches told me that my punching technique had developed a funny cycle during the previous season. He said he could tell when Tunch had been cut and then returned!

I don't think God ever intended us to walk alone. He intended us to walk with a spouse or with another believer who is a fellow warrior. There's something so dynamic about Christian warriors and brothers united, like David and Jonathan, whose souls were knitted together.

That's the true means of passing on your legacy in the life of someone else. It comes through building into someone's life.

"The power of friendship is amazing. The best ones punch through the surface and penetrate deep into the core of our souls, stopping us in our tracks."

TUNCH ILKIN
GREEN BAY PACKERS

That's what Jesus and his disciples modeled. Sure, Jesus spoke to the masses on the hills, but much of what he did was one on one, or with His three closest friends. He made disciples of the men, and then taught them how to make disciples. He didn't catch fish for them but taught them how to be fishers of men.

That's multiplication.

That's also mentoring, a valuable tool to use in the second level of role modeling. In his book *The Masculine Journey*, Robert Hicks explained, "Wherever I am on the masculine journey, I need a mentor who is at least one stage ahead of me. I need this to provide a model of masculinity at the next stage, and the encouragement I need to leave where I am and grow up a little.

"If I am a college guy enjoying the sexual pleasures women bring me, I need an older man who may be a warrior in adult life to show me how to channel or translate my sexual energy into something more constructive like business or career.

"When I'm a warrior drawing blood from everyone around me, I need a wounded man to come alongside and give me the perspective I need to see that one day, I may be the one who is bleeding.

"When I think I am bleeding to death, I need a mature man to take some pity on me, bandage my wounds, and give me the hope I need to survive."[1]

I also like what Howard Hendricks said. "Every time you build into the life of another man, you've launched a process that ideally will never end. The pedestals are empty, there's a shortage of older male examples.

"It was well expressed by a little kid in a barbershop some time ago when I asked, 'Hey, son. Whom do you want to be like?' He looked me straight in the eye and said, 'Mister, I ain't found nobody I want to be like.' Do you think he's an exception? No, there is a terrifying void of affirming maleness in our society."[2]

That point alone tells us why we need to be role models at this level. That void is there for the filling. "Most single mothers want their children to have strong positive ties with their fathers—just as all mothers do," affirmed Robyn Flans, writing in *Parent* magazine.

"But when the dads aren't available or reliable, many of these mothers feel compelled to add yet another responsibility to their already loaded schedules: seeking out a positive male role model or father figure for the children." As they seek, will they find one of us willing to help?

Such instincts, psychologists say, are right on target. Jim O'Neill, a professor of family studies at the University of Connecticut said, "Whether they're boys or girls, kids draw a sense of themselves from men and women, and the more grown-ups children know, the richer their ideas of masculinity and femininity will be."

I've talked about one athlete who stepped into the void and became an affirming person in my life. As I interviewed dozens of football players for this book, I discovered many examples of men who were willing to step out and be that level two role model for others.

Will you be one?

Keep in mind, at level two you may not be modeling *to* your kids, but you're still modeling *for* them. You are teaching your children how to reach out and impact others—how to be role models themselves.

That's a power play pay-off that's worth remembering.

And it's also worth keeping in mind as we hear a few more stories of level two success.

THE IMPACT OF A COACH

REGGIE WHITE

I think my high school coach, Robert Peerden, has been the most influential person in my life. He saw something in me that I didn't see in myself. He actually told me as a junior in high school that I had the potential to be the best defensive lineman in pro football.

I was like, how can you say something like that?

He was very instrumental in teaching me what tackling was all about, how to hang in there, how not to give up.

I listened because I respected him as a person. He cared about me and I cared about him.

He used to wrestle me and take me down and make me cry. I used to wonder why he would always do that. One day during basketball, he hit me in the chest, and I went back in the back and started crying.

He came back, and I expected him to apologize, but he said, "Until you come back and make sure you're tough, I'm going to keep doing it."

I didn't realize what he was doing until about two years ago. He tried to build some toughness in me that he didn't see in me. I took what he did to me as lessons. I didn't take it personally. And that helped me a whole lot in my career.

I kept coming back to him because I knew he cared about me as a person. He'd come over to my house and talk to me. I'd go over to his house when I had problems, sit down, and talk to him. He was twenty-six at the time, and I was eighteen. He was just like a big brother to me.

He also talked to me about God, about life in general. If I had problems, I knew I could go to him—even when I couldn't go to anybody else.

THE HELP OF AN OLDER FRIEND

MATT STOVER

A man named George Peterman taught me to turn this skinny little runt body, which supposedly I still have, because I'm in the NFL with a bunch of 250-pound guys, into a football body.

He wasn't a coach, but a friend whose son I coached in basketball. I was a Little League basketball coach for three years in high school.

He really took me under his wing, showed me how to lift weights. He was a body builder. He strengthened me up; he put ten pounds on me in one summer, which is tough to do for a skinny runt. It made me a better kicker, and if I didn't weigh what I do now, I wouldn't be in the league.

We had a great friendship. He was older, but he knew my age group, and he knew me well enough to treat me as a son and also as a friend.

You could see that genuine interest, definitely. I think if you can get a coach with a genuine interest in one of your players, it really goes a long way. It encourages you to know someone wants to really help you.

THE INSPIRATION OF A TEAMMATE

BILL BROOKS

One guy who really touched me was Daryl. We played Pop Warner football together. He was a wide receiver—a great athlete. I thought he would be in the pros.

At the time, there was this big bussing issue in Boston, where inner-city kids were being bussed out to predominantly white neighborhoods to go to school.

Well, Daryl played football for a school out in Boston, and there was racial tension there. He was playing a game one time, and his team was in a huddle. A white guy on a nearby roof shot down into the huddle with a firearm.

The bullet struck my friend Daryl in the back of the neck. Everybody just scattered, and my friend lay on the football field and couldn't move.

The bullet paralyzed him from the neck down, and he is paralyzed to this day. That hurt. Not just his football career was taken away from him, but his whole life had to change.

But the interesting thing about Daryl is that ever since that incident happened, he hasn't felt any animosity or any bitterness. He's not upset at the guy, not enemies with the guy. The guy has been forgiven. Of course, Daryl can't do certain things anymore, but he has gone on with his life. And that's touched me.

It's inspired me to be thankful for what I have and also just to do what the apostle Paul said, "Be content in whatever state you are in."

His mother is a believer, and she instilled in her children that even if those things happen, we have to forgive people no matter what they do. God is in this for a reason.

Whenever I talk to him, he's always in an upbeat mood. He's the same jokester as he was when we were younger.

Daryl's an inspiration because of his attitude—his attitude toward the whole thing, toward himself being paralyzed as a young kid with a lot of energy. He was very vibrant, good personality, good kid, didn't want to harm anybody—just out to have good, clean fun—and all this was taken away from him.

He's the kind of person who doesn't let things get him down, doesn't let anything devastate him.

Perhaps you're in a position to be such an inspiration to someone yourself. Don't underestimate the number of people around you who just might need a wise, encouraging friend to look up to—or over to.

Former University of Southern California basketball coach George Raveling has seen the need for these kinds of role models. "Lots of times the kids' role models are other kids, and that could be more dangerous," Raveling said. "The world they face is more dangerous and complicated than the one we faced in a lot of ways. It's so confrontational.

"Coaches can be more of an influence than parents or the pros. We have an awesome responsibility. A chance to have a positive influence or a negative influence or no influence.

That's why every day after practice, I give my players photocopies of articles from papers, stories about different players and their attitudes about things, just so they can understand better what it takes to achieve excellence."[3]

Legendary high school basketball coach Morgan Wooten agrees. "I've seen it all," said the third winningest coach in high school basketball history. "I started coaching in an orphanage, and I'm convinced that the real influence comes from the people who are in direct contact with these kids. Coaches, teachers, parents, peers. And athletes, if they will take the time to come in and appear in person...."[4]

The examples are numerous and the opportunities are endless. We can all make a difference in a life by offering our own as an example or inspiration—to a friend, a kid on a local team, a neighbor, or a kid at church.

Be a Tunch in somebody else's life.

LEVEL THREE MODELING:
SETTING YOUR SIGHTS ON STRANGERS

Throughout this book I make the point that the most important model our kids will have is their fathers. So it may sound contradictory when I say the most important role model some kids will ever have will be the long-distance, level three role model.

We just read George Raveling's observation that children often have no one at home to follow. When dads abdicate, level one role modeling becomes only a dream. But we must take that idea one step further. Some children, because of their environment, don't even have the direct contact level two role models to follow.

At home, there may be a war where no port is safe. At school, there may be apathy. And in the neighborhood there are only predators where role models should be.

Who will step into the void? Often a long-distance friend swoops into the life of a young person on a one-time, drop-in basis. Sometimes it's an athlete who may never meet the young person—but can help him or her just the same.

"Often children do better picking role models than adults do."

KEN RUETTGERS
GREEN BAY PACKERS

I think for the most part our children do better picking role models and sifting through their examples than we adults do. Kids have a better insight and inside track on what they glean—in both positive and negative ways.

That's a bit of comfort when we realize how much is riding on the choices the rudderless kids in our society have to make.

The influences on the third level run the gamut from writers to athletes to singers to inner-city mission workers. They cover the field from athletes with foundations to philanthropic businessmen to housewives who teach literacy.

It happened to Paul Frase through music. Paul Frase is no neglected teenager. He's a defensive lineman for the New York Jets. At a time when he himself should have been a long-distance role model, he was in dire need of that kind of example in his life.

"I was doing very few things right in 1991. In the early summer, things started to change. I knew alcohol had started to consume and control my life, and I didn't like what was happening. I knew I was hurting people along the way, and I didn't want that to happen, either.

"We came to the summer, and I was still struggling and drinking quite a bit. In August at training camp, the big come-back year for me began. I was returning from having Graves disease. Everybody was wondering if I was going to be able to come back.

"I was listening to a Steve Camp song called 'Living Dangerously.' There was a section in there where Steve says, 'Living dangerously is not living recklessly, but righteously, and it is because of God's radical grace for us that we can risk living a life of radical obedience to him.'

"At that point, I got on my knees. It was weird, I played that part of the song about six times over, and I got on my knees and asked the Lord to release the bondage that alcohol had over my life.

"From then on, alcohol wasn't that significant. I went from drinking five nights a week, to one night a week, to one night a month, then I went eight and half months without touching any alcohol at all.

"During that time, I met the woman who is now my wife. Our very first date, I guess you could call it, we were together for about ten hours, and about six and half or seven hours of that time, we talked about God."

Long-distance modeling by Steve Camp proved to be the turning point for Paul. Steve Camp probably doesn't even know Paul Frase, but he changed his life.

That's what level three role models can do if they just get involved.

We've talked a bit about Reggie White already, but let me share another thing Reggie is doing. He and his pastor, the Rev. Jerry Upton, have combined economic resources to establish a Knoxville community development bank, which in the four months since its opening had issued nearly $400,000 in loans to inner-city Knoxville residents.

Reggie said, "I've decided that what I'm doing isn't about being a role model, it is about being a responsible man.

"What I'm doing is helping my people because I can help my people, not because of some obligation simply because I'm an athlete. I'd be doing this even if I wasn't an athlete."[5]

What a lesson for us all! We don't need to be professional athletes to reach out on the third level and show the way. We need to help our people, our families, and our communities because we should, not because we have a powerful, famous platform.

"What I'm doing isn't about being a role model, it's about being a responsible man."

REGGIE WHITE
GREEN BAY PACKERS

We all qualify. Cris Carter of the Vikings said, "If you walk upright and walk with the dignity of God, and if you live and show the love, joy, peace, patience, kindness, and perseverance that God has promised in your life, people will see it. People that you don't even know will see it, and they'll see that there's something different about you.

"Even if you work a 9-to-5 job, people will see a joy, a love about you, a peace that is inside of you, and they'll know that there's something different about you. Remember the verse that says, 'He that is in me is greater than he that is in the world.'

"You can almost see it. Those who don't know God, or who might know who God is, but don't want to have anything to do with Him—they still respect a man or woman of God."

That's what we dads need to be. Men of God. Regular 9-to-5 guys who won't ever be famous, six-foot six-inch, three hundred pound guys whose name everybody knows. But we'll have the same purpose. And that's to model the love of God at home, in the community, and throughout the land.

Triple-threat men.

PERSONAL TIME-OUT

1. If my kids were to rate me on how well I'm doing as a role model to them each day, would they:
   a. Put me on waivers
   b. Put me on the disabled list
   c. Trade me for their friend's dad
   d. Name me Most Valuable Pop

What are three things I can do during the coming week to let my kids know they are as important to me as my job?

2. How am I a role model to the following people in level two?
   a. My co-workers
   b. My neighbors
   c. My golfing, racquetball, or other sports partners
   d. My accountability group or friends at church

3. What can I do the next time I am with these people to model Christ in a compelling way?

4. If I'm not a well-known athlete, how can I develop third-level role modeling situations? Is there a community outreach center where I can volunteer? Are there kids I can help through coaching or by being a Big Brother?

5. Which people influenced me most on each level? How can I learn from and multiply their effectiveness in others today?

RUETTGERS' REFLECTIONS

Football truths that also work in real life

Are you the hammer or the nail?

The "I got my guy" mentality is a losing mentality.

CHAPTER SIX

A Father's Arsenal

I am most influenced in my life by my diving coach.
She is like a sister to me.

—TEENAGE ATHLETE

Imagine this. It's a late-season Sunday, and the Green Bay Packers have a huge conference showdown with the Chicago Bears at Lambeau Field. All year we've battled for position, and now it's down to one game.

We file into the locker room as usual. Each of us goes through his pre-game ritual: getting taped and dressed, receiving some pre-game treatments for aches and pains, psyching ourselves up, and waiting to meet with the coaching staff to discuss the game plan before hitting the field.

But then something strange happens. Coach calls us together and says, "Men, today I'm trying something different. We're scrapping our game plan for this contest. I know we've been working on it all week, but we're just going to hope for the best. You'll figure out what to do once you get out there on the field. You'll learn from your mistakes, and I'm sure everything will come out okay."

That coach had better have reservations for the next flight out of town. He would have the support of absolutely no one in the organization—from the owner down to the guy sitting in the cheap seats in the end zone.

It's ludicrous to think of playing an NFL football game without a plan.

The Green Bay Packers could end up looking like a bunch of school-yard kids. Yet how often do we as dads face our job as father without a clue as to how we're going to get the job done?

For years, a sign hung in our locker room that spelled out the importance of taking the time to strategize. Although it was directed to us as football players, it fits for us as dads, too. "Failure to plan," the sign said, "is planning to fail."

In football, coaches begin their strategizing soon after the last game of the season—if not before. Same with our plans for what we plan to accomplish as parents. The best time to start proper role modeling is when our kids are very young—or even before they're born.

Do you remember the story of David Williams? David plays right tackle for the Houston Oilers. A few years ago, he was the focus of the nation's attention—for attending the birth of his first child.

What made the story unusual, though, was the fact that the Houston Oilers schedule-makers didn't take into account his wife's due date. The baby decided to arrive at the same time Williams would normally have been on a road trip with his teammates.

So Williams opted to miss the team's trip. The Oilers docked his pay, and Williams became an overnight hero with wives everywhere.

What David Williams really did was demonstrate some great modeling for his little boy—before he was even born.

"If it came up again, I would do the same thing," he said. "I never regretted one minute of staying behind with her and my child. I hope he'll look back on it and say, 'Dad stayed behind for me. Turned down a big paycheck to be there for me and mom.'

"I hope it instills in him the values and how important family is. I hope it's something he'll thrive on when he gets older and he starts having a family of his own."

It may be best to start that early, but some of us are looking for strategies, power plays, that will work just a little bit later in life. Regardless of where we are on the timeline, though, the best time to begin is now.

How can you maximize your home field advantage early on?

We've talked about the "Daddy Sneak"—slow and steady gains. And the "Triple Threat"—maximizing your sphere of influence. But now it's time for "A Father's Arsenal"—an array of tactics that will help change your kid's score, and your own.

This is called a father's arsenal, perhaps. But these are kid-tested, mother-approved strategies:

STRATEGY 1: MAKE YOUR HOME A SAFE HAVEN— THAT WILL TRAVEL

You can't imagine how good it feels to come home to Lambeau Field after a road trip to some enemy territory such as Soldier Field or that noisy Silverdome. Our home field may not be the greatest football edifice in the league, but it's our safe haven.

Here we can be fairly confident (don't tell Coach I said that) because we're on friendly ground. Our fans, for the most part, cheer us on. They don't yell mindless, sarcastic things at us (most of the time). They don't suggest awful places that we should go (most of the time). They don't try to make us reconsider our calling to be football players (most of the time).

They encourage us. They love us. They make football fun again (most of the time).

Our kids need a place like that.

Home might be the only safe haven our children have to protect themselves from the cold indifference — or evil— of the world. As dads, we must take the lead in making home a retreat.

Sometimes that safe haven for our kids extends outside the home. That's because a true haven lies within a parent's heart. It is comprised of an attitude of concern for our kids. And it travels with us wherever we go.

Author Steve Farrar has experienced this. He attended a luncheon of pro athletes I was invited to, and he brought his son, Josh, along with him.

As we sat around the table with some of the most incredible athletes in the NFL, I asked Josh, "How old are you?"

He told us how old he was.

I said, "What grade are you in?"

He said, "Fifth grade."

One of the other athletes said, "Fifth Grade! Aren't you supposed to be in sixth grade?"

Because Josh was a guest of mine at the table, I tried in that quick instant to think of the right words to say. Before I could respond, his father, Steve said, "Well, that's because Josh's dad started him late."

That was all that was needed. The conversation continued in a different direction.

Steve Farrar had provided safety for his son in an awkward situation.

When I asked Steve about the incident later, he vaguely remembered the conversation and couldn't even recall his response. It was as natural for him to provide safety for his son as it is for a baseball player to spit.

You can spit too, I bet.

STRATEGY 2:
DON'T TREAT YOUR KIDS THE SAME

There's a unique relationship between dads and daughters and between dads and sons. We don't treat them the same. And ideally, we shouldn't.

Kids need gender-specific love and attention. And since male-oriented advice already dominates this book—naturally—let's focus for the most part on daughters.

I try to spend some one-on-one time with each of my daughters (and my son) before they go to bed every night—reading to them or listening to them read, praying with them, and talking about the day.

When we sit around the dinner table at night, everybody gets an opportunity to talk.

Something else I try to do is take each of my daughters out for a date once every couple of weeks. (I make it a point to take Matt out for special outings as well.) My older daughter, Katherine, is just five years old. But she knows that the way I treat her at five years old is how I expect the boy she's dating in ten to twelve years to treat her.

Even though this doesn't dominate our conversation, it comes up occasionally. It's a perfect time to start building into her life what to expect of a man. So I try to model the respect and honor she should look for down the line during courtship.

Kicker Mike Horan put it like this: "My daughters are going to look for a husband that has the same qualities that I do."

Scary? Or reassuring? We'll always have a strong impact on our girls, whether it be good or bad. This continues all the way through the teenage years. If you don't think so, ask your wife

If you don't recognize the legacy your wife's father left in her heart, talk to her about it. She'll remember. Eventually a dad's input in his daughter's life surfaces—for better or worse.

In fact, you've probably seen evidence of some of your father-in-law's character traits in how your wife interacts with you.

The words of a favorite Wayne Watson song speak to a father's bittersweet long for his daughter to grow up and find happiness.

It's called, "Somewhere in the World."

> Somewhere in the world today, a little girl will go out to play,
> All dressed up in mama's clothes, at least that's the way I suppose it goes.
> Somewhere in the world tonight, before she reaches to turn out the light,
> She'll be praying from a tender heart, this simple prayer that's a work of art.
> And I don't even know her name, but I'm praying for her just the same.
> That the Lord will write his name upon her heart,
> Because somewhere in the course of this life, my little boy will need a godly wife.
> So hold onto Jesus, baby, wherever you are.
> Somewhere in the world out there, that little girl is learning how to care,
> She's picking up her mama's charm, or maybe swinging around in her daddy's arms.
> Somewhere in the world to be, though the future is not real clear to me,
> Theirs could be a tender love, founded in eternal love above,

And I don't even know her name,
But I'm praying for her just the same,
That the Lord will write his name upon her heart,
'Cause somewhere in the course of his life, a little boy will meet a godly wife.
So hold onto Jesus, baby, wherever you are."[1]

Lomas Brown of the Detroit Lions is one huge guy. He's six-foot four-inches and weighs about 290 pounds. But when I talked to him about his three daughters and how he feels about them, it was easy to see who holds his big heart.

He loves to go out with Antoinette, Ashley, and Adrienne.

"I want to have our lines of communication open," Lomas says of his daughters. "I don't want them to be afraid to come tell me anything. So I have to let them know that in so many ways. That's why we spend a lot of time together—just me and the girls.

"On Mondays and Wednesdays, I go pick them up from school, and a lot of times we don't go straight home. We go somewhere and eat. We'll do a lot of talking then about how school was and what's going on. That's good for me."

I can imagine it causes quite a stir when the big guy walks into a McDonald's with his little girls in tow. But I can also imagine how special those three daughters of Lomas and Dolores Brown feel about those times out with Dad.

There's nothing wrong with girls and baseball. Or girls who love to wrestle and dig in dirt. I'm not advocating chauvinism, here, guys. But a good strategy for role modeling is to reinforce your children's unique gender tendencies as they manifest themselves. That might mean love of talk, love of dance, or love of McDonald's.

Nothing can make a little girl feel more sure of feminine success than Dad's interest and praise.

HALFTIME POINTERS

Dad's a Fun Guy

➢ Make your home a fun haven. Remember, if children don't feel their home is kid-friendly, it won't matter if it's kid safe—they'll just hang out somewhere else. A fun home has laughter, music, spontaneity, friendly supervision, the joy of the Lord, and probably ice cream in the freezer. How well are you stocked?

➢ Propose a Family's Choice day. One morning, surprise your family with the announcement that you'll spend the day with them—doing whatever they want to do. It might work best to break the day down into parts so everyone has some say. Only two rules: everyone but Dad has a say, and everybody sticks together all day.

➢ Create a family time capsule. What do you want to say to the world long after you're gone? Fill a metal box with pictures, letters, odds and ends—whatever gets the message across. Then bury it in the backyard (too deep for Fido to dig up).

STRATEGY 3:
DON'T LET 'EM TAG ALONG—TAKE 'EM PLACES

Try to take your children along with you wherever you go, whenever you're able to do so. I take my children if I need to stop by the stadium. They love that.

Or if the offensive line is going out for dinner, I try to take one of my children with me. Usually the other offensive linemen don't mind. It not only sets an example for our children, but it sets an example for those around us. They can see where we place our priorities.

I like taking my kids to work. It doesn't matter that I'm a professional athlete; they don't know the difference. I encourage dads to take their kids to work when they can, because no matter what your work is, they get a chance to see what you do. It's a great field trip.

My daughter enjoys having me take her to ballet. Just the fact that I am taking her to ballet demonstrates to her that she is significant. This kind of thing is something we can all do.

My dad used to take me golfing with his buddies. I didn't play golf much. I mostly raked sand traps, tended the flag, and did a little caddying, but I was there. And his buddies became, in some ways, role models. I've kept in contact over the years with them, all of them dear friends.

I was lucky to have a father who would involve me in his friendships and very blessed that he chose such quality men to be friends with. Not only were they good examples to me, the experience still helps me seek out friends with strong characters.

And it wouldn't have happened if Dad hadn't let me tag along with him.

On a flight home from Dallas one time, I met a Texan who told me that he takes his family into the inner city. They go once a month to serve families there. He said that not only were the people he served blessed, but his family was even more blessed.

What a great strategy this tagging along thing is!

STRATEGY 4: BE A FACE IN THE CROWD

The next time you go to one of your kids' sporting events, notice who's there to watch. It seems that some kids always have mom and dad there. And some kids just get dropped off.

Drop-off kids. They get dropped off for school. Dropped off for T-Ball. Dropped off for day care. Dropped off at church (if they go at all). Dropped off in life.

I can't imagine anything worse than being a drop-off kid. That's why we as dads have to make a point to be there when life happens for our kids.

Being there doesn't simply mean being there physically. It means mentally, emotionally, and spiritually. You can be there in person but still not pay attention. So it's important to put aside your own concerns and set aside time for closeness.

I think the most important feeling that kids can have is to know that their parents support them in their endeavors. There's something about a father just being there, not necessarily at the front of the stage, not yelling at a coach. Just being a wonderful face in the crowd.

My dad was always there. I knew. I didn't always know exactly where he was, but I knew he was in the stands when I played football.

When I was a Boy Scout, he didn't like backpacking or camping. His idea of camping out was to make reservations at a hotel with a soft mattress, a hot shower, and a good golf course next door.

So he compensated. For almost every Boy Scout camping trip we took, he'd make sure to drive me to the camp, pick me up, or both. That was support, and it meant a lot to me.

Now, it's my turn. I need to be present whenever I can at my children's activities. I don't have to coach. I don't have to yell or scream or cheer. Just the fact that I'm taking the time to be there tells my kids that they're important—and worth watching.

David Williams, the guy who was modeling for his daughter before she was born, must have learned it from his dad. "My dad never missed a game from the time I started junior high school to the time I got to be a Houston Oiler," he recalls.

You see, dads? It's your face in the crowd that your kid wants to see— and will remember.

STRATEGY 5:
IF YOU CAN'T BE THERE—BE FELT

Perhaps you're a dad who would give anything to be with your children as they compete, perform, and grow up. But you can't. Perhaps it's a custodial problem. Perhaps it's a distance difficulty.

For whatever reason, you and your children are separated, and you feel as if you might be cheating them.

With communications so advanced these days, you can find a way to let them know you're thinking of them. Try these tips: Drop a post card. Make a ten-minute call. Draw a quick picture with a short note and either FAX it home or send it E-mail.

If the separation is more long-term, perhaps this would help. Keep a journal and write down your feelings about your kids. Tell your children what you're doing that day, how you wish they were with you, and that you're thinking about them.

Photocopy it and mail it to them if you can. If you can't get it to them now, save the journal and give it to your kids when their hearts are open and ready for it.

San Diego Charger kicker John Carney knows what this is all about. His young son lives with his mother, so Carney is often separated from him.

When they do get together, Carney says, "I try to spend as much time with him as I possibly can, and that's turned out to be about three or four days a week. But it's still not enough. I always want more."

Carney has a lot to share with his boy. "I remember a lot of things that I learned growing up, from coaches or my father or neighbors. I want to pass these experiences on to my son.

"I want to be there the first time he strikes out in Little League, or the first time he catches a fish. And if I have a word of wisdom that could make a difference in his life and help him be a better Christian, then I want to give it."

STRATEGY 6:
TELL IT LIKE IT IS—AND THE WAY IT SHOULD BE.

Children don't learn how to make right choices by osmosis. We can't assume that just because they're living in a Christian family they will be equipped to fight off the vast assortment of bad choices that are on today's menu.

Josh McDowell has been keeping track of the choices kids are making today, and the findings are not all that encouraging. "In early 1994," he said, "we surveyed thousands of kids ages eleven through eighteen and asked them 193 questions.

"More than 80 percent of those surveyed attended an evangelical church weekly and 86 percent said they had made a commitment to trust Christ as their Savior and Lord. What the survey told us is that many of our kids are not adopting our values system at all. In addition, 66 percent said they had lied to their parents or another adult in the last three months. Almost that many, 59 percent, had lied to their peers. At least 45 percent watched MTV at least once a week."

Josh continued, "In past decades, children grew up in an atmosphere that communicated absolute standards for behavior. Certain things were right and certain things were wrong. A child's parents, teachers, ministers, youth workers, and other adults all have held these standards.

"...Today's culture reflects philosophies of 'if it feels good, do it' and 'if it works for you, why not?' Instead of hearing the words 'right and wrong,' from Hollywood, Nashville, and Madison Avenue, our children get bombarded with hours of images and sounds that glamorize immortality and mock biblical values."

I think I know where the basic breakdown lies. It's in our homes. I think we need to tell our children of the benefits of the right choices, the consequences of the wrong choices. We need to do it in an honest way, and we need to take time to do it the correct way.

How can you equip your children with the truth? Help them put on "the full armor of God," which includes the "belt of truth," as Paul described in Ephesians 6. So that when the day of evil comes—and believe me, it's already here—they may be able to stand their ground.

There are different ways we can teach our children the truth. Natural consequence is one. If we try to tell children that they should be careful climbing a tree, that's one thing. But if they unfortunately fall and twist an ankle because they were fooling around, they'll learn the lesson even better.

Logical consequences that we set beforehand and enforce are another method. In this regard, we need to stick to our guns and be consistent. We need to make sure our children ask for forgiveness and experience sorrow when they're wrong.

Of course, if we're truly the role models as fathers that we're supposed to be, then we'll also have the humility and courage to say "I'm sorry, will you forgive me?" when we do wrong. There's great power in the phrase "will you forgive me?"

My son is now seven. I think it's getting close to the time to talk with my son about another truth: God's wonderful and beautiful plan for how husbands and wives create a family.

If I don't tell him soon, someone else will. Kids know more at a younger age these days. I want my children to know the truth about God's plan based on His Word, not on secondhand knowledge, incomplete knowledge, or knowledge based on the wrong set of morals taught by a second grade classmate.

Another way we help our kids make right choices is by modeling holiness. In the New Testament, Peter wrote, "Do not conform to the evil desires you had when you lived in ignorance. But just as he who called you is holy, so be holy in all you do; for it is written: 'Be holy, because I am holy'" (I Peter 1: 14-16).

STRATEGY 7:
PUT RELATIONSHIPS FIRST, RULES SECOND

Rules without relationships lead to rebellion.

I think that principle is at the heart of what the Apostle Paul is saying in Ephesians 6:4. "Fathers, do not exasperate your children; instead bring them up in the training and instruction of the Lord."

When it comes to setting rules and enforcing them around the house, resentment reigns unless a loving relationship has already been established. Kids grow angry when we pound them with rules without tempering that with a godly, loving foundation.

Colossians 3:21 suggests that the only thing we accomplish by enforcing rules without relationship is to discourage our children. That's because kids respond negatively if they don't trust us to do what's best for them.

If we lay down the law in our house but haven't developed a strong relationship with our children, those laws are worthless and hollow. But if we enjoy a strong bond with our kids, then there's a basis for the rules that we set in our household.

How can you show your kids that you care more about them than you do about rules?

STRATEGY 8:
KNOW THY KID—BETTER THAN BASS FISH

While attending a Christian conference for NFL husbands and wives, I sat down for lunch with Mo Lewis, a linebacker for the New York Jets. As we ate, we began talking about our interests. I remember thinking how tempted I'd been to bring the materials for this book along to work on at the conference.

As I talked with Mo, I found out that he had a far different interest. He loves bass fishing, and he'd brought along his bass fishing magazines to the conference. He was excited to tell us all about the ins and outs. He knew what kind of boat to use, what lures to use, and he knew the best type of waters to fish.

While listening to him, I found myself thinking, *Boy, if we could only get to know our children like we get to know our hobbies! If we could know our kids like he knew bass!*

"Listening is the main thing. Listening to what God wants, listening to what your wife and kids need and want."

KARL MECKLENBURG
DENVER BRONCOS

If we could "catch" our children like Mo could hook a fish, we could answer many of the questions we have about our families. Our kids could tell us lots about who they are, what they need. We just need to tune into their thinking.

There may be no fail-safe way to do that, but the best method I can think of is to communicate with them. And I don't mean one-way communication. I mean spending as much time listening to them as talking to them.

Karl Mecklenburg has some good advice on listening. "I think listening is the main thing. Listening to what God wants, listening to what your wife and kids need and want.

"I had a real tendency to go out and charge ahead and not take the time to understand what other people wanted or what God wanted. It was just go, go, go."

If we want to know our kids, we have to listen—and go slow. Slow down and really probe. What did my daughter just say? What does this mean about her self-image?

Are you ready for this strategy? You might discover that fathering beats fishing any day. And kids, especially yours, are more interesting than most bass.

STRATEGY 9:
PUMP 'EM UP

Think of the impact of our words. Words of love breed feelings of comfort, security, and self-worth. Words of hate result in feelings of uneasiness, fear, and worthlessness. Which feelings would we rather foster among the people whose lives we touch?

Think of those times in your life when all you want to do is live to please God. Did you ever stop to realize that our kids, in a similar way, are focused on pleasing us as fathers?

I can tell this is true when my children bring home an art project from school. They slam the door open, rush into the house, and excitedly place their masterpiece in my hands. For them, the fun part of doing an art project and bringing it home is to see their dad's reaction.

Kids thrive on the encouragement we give them.

Conversely there's little that can be as harmful as ignoring our children or withholding deserved compliments. That discouragement remains with them for a long time.

The best approach is to catch our children doing something right and praise them for it, rather than trying to catch them doing things wrong and criticize them. We need to be quick to praise and slow to criticize.

It doesn't have to be elaborate, either. No amount of kudos or applause thrills my kids as much those attaboys they receive from their father. I know that in the arena of sports, the attaboys are some of the greatest motivators you can give athletes.

Typically, those motivators are far more influential and more powerful than money. "Attaboy" praises make your children feel recognized, significant. It's a great way for a father to pump up his kids. And if you do it in front of their friends—that's an added bonus.

Any chance I get, I tell my kids they're being great leaders.

Encouragement can create a leader.

Matt Stover became a leading kicker in the NFL because of the encouragement of his father. "He was encouraging the whole time," Matt says of his dad. "It was like he was a coach, but he wasn't a coach. He was the encouragement side of the game. He kept things going."

Will our children remember us as people whose encouragement "kept things going"?

STRATEGY 10:
LET LOVE GO UNDEFEATED

Do you remember the *Field of Dreams* spoof commercial in the 1995 Super Bowl? A young man in his mid-thirties walks out of the famous Iowa farmhouse, across the lawn, and onto that majestic baseball diamond plowed out of the cornfields.

In the distance, an older baseball player emerges out of the cornfields and greets the young man.

It's his father.

His father asks him to pass him a Coke. When the son reaches into the ice chest and throws his dad a discount cola, the father looks at him with disappointment and asks, "Son, why didn't you give me a Coca-Cola?"

His son answers, "Dad, isn't that great? I saved five cents!"

His father responds in disgust, "All this to save five cents?" As he turns, he throws the cola and walks away—back into the cornfield from which he came.

That commercial got rave reviews for its drama, but I think it has a secondary value in its portrayal of conditional love.

We often give our children and other loved ones affection and love only when we feel they deserve it. We fail to show them the unconditional love God has for us. God's love can't be defeated or nullified. We can never foul out.

If we accept our children unconditionally as God accepts us, then our children will learn to accept themselves. They will have a positive and healthy sense of self-worth, and they'll be able to overcome the "I must win, I must be significant trap."

In fact, our kids already know what unconditional love is — and they sure know how to give it. After a football game, my kids don't care if I win or lose, they still love me.

I want to love them in the same way. I want to keep reminding them with words and actions that God doesn't make junk, and they're loved with no strings attached.

Unfortunately for Steve Tasker and the other Buffalo Bills who suffered through losing four straight Super Bowls, they've had many chances to learn about unconditional love.

Tasker used one of those losses to his advantage. "After the second Super Bowl, I brought my five-year-old down on the field with me. I told him, 'Even though we lost the game and even though I'm very serious about football, I'll always love you and I'll never forget about you.' I wanted him to know that no matter what happened in football, it would never affect the way I felt about him. He still remembers that."

Something author Stu Weber said strikes me as appropriate here. When he first saw his newborn son, he told him, "You are mine and I am yours. And there is nothing that you could ever do to change that." Now, more than twenty years later, Stu still tells his son the same thing.

I've tried to make it a special point with my kids to let them know that I love them because they're my kids. My son knows I love him because he's my son; my daughters know I love them because they're my daughters.

How can you help your kids feel loved? Do they feel free to come to you no matter what they've done? Let them know that, even if it gets tackled now, your love can't ever be defeated.

STRATEGY 11:
JUST HUG 'EM

It's sometimes surprising to see how much hugging goes on during a football game. We're big, muscle-bound, macho men (at least that's the way people see us). Yet after a big play or a big win, there are group hugs all around.

If big, mean-looking guys can hug each other in front of glaring TV cameras, then why do we—I mean we dads of all sizes, colors, and kinds—often find it hard to hug our kids in the confines of our own homes?

When was the last time you gave your kids the kind of affectionate hug that translates into making them feel flat out suffocated in love?

According to a *USA Today* article, "Physical affection and warmth toward kids strongly predicted closer marriages and friendships...better mental health and more work success."[2]

In fact, studies have shown that infant children can die without hugs. Of course, that's not going to happen with our kids. But something in them will die if we dads don't show them some good affection.

How about it? Have you hugged your kid today?

PERSONAL TIME-OUT

1. What are three things I can do today that show my kids that our home—including my heart toward them—is the safest place on earth?

2. Am I sure that each of my children who have reached the age of accountability have put their faith and trust in Jesus Christ? If not, how can I help lead them toward that decision?

3. How much time have I spent with my children in the past week? If I don't know, am I willing to chart it out and find out for sure? How can I spend more time or more focused time?

4. Where have I taken my kids recently that I didn't have to? Where might I plan to take them so they can observe me as I interact with others?

5. Have I made choices this week that are helping me be a good example to my kids? What are some bad choices I have made that I need to repent of and perhaps even ask forgiveness for?

6. If my kids rated me on my parenting on a scale of one to ten, what number would they give me for positive, encouraging parenting? What positive steps do I need to take?

7. If my kids heard me speak at a banquet about being a parent, would they conclude that I was honest or a hypocrite?

8. How well do I display a love that can't be defeated? What part of life with kids gets me sacked nonetheless?

Who loves me today in the way I love my kids? What do they do that tells me this?

RUETTGERS' REFLECTIONS

Football truths that also work in real life

For a team to be effective, each player needs to be pulling on the same end of the rope.

All you can ask is for a player to give everything he has.

If you lose your composure in the battle, you'll lose the war.

Nothing great comes easy.

Don't forget to enjoy the game.

If you don't know your assignment, you can't carry out your assignment.

PART THREE

Inside Moves: Shaping the Soul of a Role Model

CHAPTER SEVEN

Working Out with God

My role model is my Lord and Savior Jesus Christ. He is the most perfect person to follow and idolize because He forgives you for your sins and leads you in the right direction.

Soft. Nobody who calls himself an athlete wants to be described with that word. When a player is called "soft," it means someone thinks he lacks the courage to make the big play. Or it means he isn't the "go-to" guy the team needs.

It could also mean that the player has layers of blubber where muscle is supposed to be. While he should've been in the weight room lifting the barbells, he was at McDonald's lifting the burgers.

A soft player is not ready when the whistle blows and the ball is kicked off. He is a liability to his team. He doesn't have the muscle tone needed to hand out the hits, bumps, and slamming bodies his team needs.

He misses tackles or gets shoved out of the way when he's blocking. To put it in the clearest terms I know, he's a waste of a uniform.

It's sad see a player who is talented enough to play in the NFL lose his spot on the team because he's too soft. But I know something that is a lot more tragic: When a dad can't get the job done because he's soft spiritually.

A soft Christian gets that way for the same reasons a soft football player gets to be All-Flab instead of All-Pro. Poor spiritual training.

How much better if we put forth the effort to get in shape spiritually. Then, when the really tough times come, we'll be able to respond as we should. There's a big difference between true Christian example and putting up a façade. Being a Christian is a way of life.

THE WIDE WORLD OF WIMPS

Real men are spiritual men. And real role models are spiritually strong.

I'm not alone in this thinking. Notice what writer Tommy Evans said, "It's painfully apparent that America is losing its families. I'm convinced the primary cause of this national crisis is the 'feminization' of the American male. When I say feminization, I'm not talking about sexual preference, I'm trying to describe a misunderstanding of manhood that has produced a nation of "sissy-fied" men who abdicate their roles of spiritually pure leaders, thus forcing women to fill the vacuum.

"...How do we break the cycle? By getting men to assume their responsibilities and take back the reigns of spiritually pure leadership God intended us to hold. We must become real spiritually directed men once again—pure in our passions and our priorities."[1]

The existence of so many spiritually "soft" men reinforces the old stereotype that Christian men are wimps. When I wanted to find a friend in the faith, a Barnabus among some of the Christians on my brother's college campus, even he told me, "Ken, those guys are a bunch of wimps."

To some extent, I had to agree. But God didn't call us to be wimps as Christians. I realize it's a tough decision to hang tough as a man of God in this culture. Yet I don't think we have to look far to find men who are tough—both spiritually and in their life's work.

Think about the football players whose stories I'm sharing in this book. You wouldn't dare call Reggie White a wimp. Or Tunch Ilkin. Or Anthony Muñoz. The world of sports is a showcase of powerhouse men who are stand-up guys for God. They know how to stay in shape physically and spiritually.

Look at these stats from the George Gallop Polling Agency. "Recent Gallop surveys report that by a margin of 46 percent to 38 percent, women are more likely than men to attend religious services in the past week. What's more, by a margin of 57 percent to 37 percent, women are more likely than men to say they give serious and consistent attention to the development of their faith."[2]

While we can be glad that women in our country are so dedicated to God, we cannot be satisfied with these numbers. Like a half-time report from the coaching staff that proves we've been sloughing off, this Gallop survey should wake us up to the fact that a comeback is in order.

As we hit the faith workout room, another voice of challenge belongs to Matt Millen. The NFL-great-turned broadcaster gives us his best spiritual Howard Cosell monologue when he says, "I have a hard time with wimpy Christians. I can't stand it."

The words of Tom Petersburg, chaplain of the Cleveland Browns, have the shock value of truth we need. "The average Christian male wants enough of Jesus to make him successful, but not enough to interfere with his own selfish agenda."

Indeed, until we make our agenda line up with God's, we'll never have the strength, power, and dynamic faith to make a difference in this world.

CALLING ALL MEN

As I look around the locker room of the Green Bay Packers, I see men who are physically strong, tough, durable, and some would say...studly.

We play a very "manly" game. It takes commitment, courage, strength, discipline, and heart. But we don't get this far on our own or grow to be giant men by choice. We were blessed with the physical tools necessary to compete at this level.

"It takes more courage, strength, sacrifice, heart, and commitment to be a man of God than to be a man of the NFL."

KEN RUETTGERS
GREEN BAY PACKERS

But as I continue to look around, I notice that some of us "real men" don't have what it takes to be a godly husband and father.

Although I respect my profession and have admiration for the fraternity of football players, I realize it takes much more courage, strength, sacrifice, heart, and commitment to be a man of God than it does to be a man of the NFL.

Each spring at the NFL combines, all the top college players show up to be measured, weighed, time, probed, and observed. This way the pro scouts can judge their skill level and perceived value in the National Football League.

Maybe it would help us dads as well to check up on our commitment to Christ. So here's a quick spiritual combine, a chance to test your spiritual fitness.

WHAT DRIVES YOUR FAITH?

1. A HOLY FIRE — OR FIRE INSURANCE?

We've all heard salvation referred to as fire insurance—a policy that guarantees we'll go to heaven rather than to hell. It's a very shallow way of looking at what Jesus has done for us. But for some, this is really the way they see it—and the way they live.

In his book *Strong Men in Tough Times*, Edwin Lewis Cole examined the way many church members live. "Ten percent cannot be found, 20 percent never attend, 25 percent never pray, 30 percent never read the Bible, 40 percent never give to the church, 60 percent never give to world missions, 75 percent never assume a ministry service in the church, 95 percent have never won a person to Christ, yet 100 percent expect to go to heaven."

If we're doing nothing for the kingdom of God but waiting for Him to take us to heaven, then our commitment is weak. Are you living a full-blown life of fiery faith—or waiting on a ladder, safe but ineffective?

2. STEADY STAMINA — OR SHALLOW SPRINTS?

If you've ever been in a workout gym during the first week of January you've noticed that the place is packed. Ninety percent of the people in there have made New Year's resolutions and they're making good on them.

But come back a week later. You may just have the place to yourself. Each week throughout the month, there are fewer and fewer people in the gym. By February you no longer have to wait in line to use a machine or get a spot on the bench press. The average New Year's resolution lasts less than a week.

Are you trying to get by as a New Year's Resolution Christian?

We need to be men who aren't that fickle with our commitment to God. The Christian life is not a 100-yard dash, but a marathon. It's the race of the tortoise, not the hare. It takes consistency and resolve to build a life of faith one day at a time.

But it takes something else, too. Gutting it up rarely works. You need stamina *and* the Holy Spirit to help you make real changes. That's the difference between the race of substance and the sporadic sprint.

It's not how you start that's vital, but how you finish. Even many of the Bible characters we admire stumbled. But we have to ask: Did they get back up and continue? Were they seeking God until the end?

Are you?

3. WILLING CHANGE—OR BLOCKED GAINS?

God has already done something for us who've been saved by trusting Jesus. The next question is whether we're willing to let Him keep working in us.

Eugene Robinson of the Seattle Seahawks is one of those strong football players who tells it like it is. "When you come into a personal relationship with Jesus Christ," Robinson said, "God starts changing things. He says, 'I know nobody sees this, but I don't like it. Get rid of it.'"

This guy knows that to be a righteous man he has to submit to God. He's got to be willing to say, "I don't like that either, that's not consistent. Let's get rid of that."

"God says in his Word that he who began a good work in you will complete it until the day of Christ Jesus," Robinson continued. "God is continually making you more and more like Christ, and using every situation and circumstance that you're involved in to accomplish that goal. When you meet a holy God in that fashion, I don't care what state you're in, it's going to force you to change.

"God is going to deal with you intimately and on a personal basis, just as he deals with me. ...Yes, there are consequences for your sins, but God's going to deal with you on a personal basis. He is directly interested in making you more and more like Jesus Christ. When you become a

Christian, you'd better be ready. Don't do any half-stepping, jiving around. This is the real deal.

"If we were dealing with a sin issue, I could fool you with great language and an exterior that looks really good. But when you open the box, you might say, 'He's a jerk, he treats his wife badly, and his language is foul.'

"When you become a Christian, you'd better be ready. Don't do any half-stepping, jiving around. This is the real deal."

EUGENE ROBINSON
SEATTLE SEAHAWKS

"But when God opens that box, He sees stuff that nobody sees, and He goes way below the surface, and He says, 'I'm going to deal with you. I've been there. You can't get away from Me.'

"The world can't see that, and I don't think the world is ready for that."

Come to think about it, are we ready for that?

One day when I'm held accountable in front of God, I doubt that He'll review my game films. But He will review the game from my life. He won't focus on the penalties I've received, He'll focus on the man of God that I was or wasn't. How I loved Him with all my heart and how I loved others as I loved myself.

How much better off we are if we let God work in us now so that when we stand before Him, we'll come with a good report.

Are you letting God take new ground in you—or blocking the gains He could make in your life?

4. A TRUE VIEW — OR A SKEWED VIEW?

Often we relate to God in light of our relationship with our parents. If your parents were loving and supportive, it's easier for you to believe in a loving, merciful God. But if your parents were demanding and harsh, you may likewise imagine you can never do enough to please God.

Of course, God possesses all of the characteristics of a good parent and none of a bad one. That just means that if our parents demonstrated negative traits, we may have to work harder to develop a truer view of God.

In the meantime, we also play a major role in forming our children's view of God.

HALFTIME POINTERS

Team up with God

➢ Trust the basics. You're responsible for giving your children a spiritual education. Are you taking advantage of these time-tested opportunities;

➢ Church; family devotions; Bible-based videos and tapes; bedtime prayers; everyday teachable moments; Bible memory.

➢ Pray specifically. Do you pray for your children throughout the day? Try to enter kid-important events in your appointment book or journal to pray about in a specific way. For example: "10:30—Joel has an English test."

➢ Take spiritual risks. Don't brush difficult questions or Scripture passages under the rug. Wonder aloud about what you don't understand about your faith. Let your kids see that the truth isn't fragile and that the Christian life is a learning adventure. By so doing, you'll be modeling a deep trust in God.

God alone can be trusted at all times and in all circumstances. That's a tough thing to accept when we realize how many people we *want* to totally trust but can't or couldn't. It can skew our view of God. The truth is that He alone possesses the power to deliver on every promise He makes.

Gladys Aylward was missionary to China more than fifty years ago. During World War II, she was forced to flee when the Japanese invaded Yang Cheng. With only one assistant to help her, she led more than one hundred orphans over the mountain top and then across more mountains toward free China.

In their book *The Hidden Price of Greatness*, Ray Besson and Ranelda Mackhunsicker recount a great story of Gladys's trust in God. "During Gladys' harrowing journey out of war torn Yang Cheng...she grappled with despair as never before. After passing a sleepless night, she faced the morning with no hope of reaching safety. A 13-year-old girl in the group reminded her of their much-loved story of Moses and the Israelites crossing the Red Sea.

"'But I'm not Moses,' Gladys cried in desperation.

"'Of course you aren't.' the girl said, 'But Jehovah is still God.'"

The God of Moses of long ago is the same God who watched over Gladys Aylward fifty years ago and the same God who takes care of pro football players—and fathers the world over—today.

Is that how your heart views God?

5. TUXEDO RESPECT — OR T-SHIRT FLIPPANCY?

God is indeed good, but God must also be feared in the proper way. In the past few years, I've noticed the popularity of "No Fear" shirts. These shirts should say "No Fear Except of God."

As we seek to understand God, we need the biblical perspective that wisdom begins with the fear of God (Psalm 111:10). He wants us to be courageous warriors, but He also wants us to have the proper respect and reverence for Him.

Former Washington Redskins head coach Joe Gibbs, as quoted in *Life* magazine, said, "Each morning I ask myself, what can I take credit for in my life? I really think about that. The answer is almost nothing. Even though I can take credit for almost nothing, I can do all things through Christ. That's where my power comes from."

Imagine the joy the Father experiences when we give Him the glory, awe, and respect He so richly deserves.

Do you fear God in the proper way? Or are you dressed in the right outfit—but wearing the wrong slogan on your life?

NOW THAT YOU KNOW THE SCORE

The combines are over, the results are in. You know where you need to improve. You know just how you stack up against veteran pros. You may even know what draft pick you would be.

But there are several things you can still do to improve your position —things that could make or break you in the league. Some people call them fundamentals, others calls them the keys to a shut-out:

STUDY THE PLAYBOOK

Perhaps you remember the commotion that was caused a few years ago when a professional athlete lost his playbook. Because of its intriguing possibilities, it was the talk of the sports world for a couple days.

Imagine the consternation it caused the coaching staff to know that their carefully designed plays were now open for public inspection—and open to scrutiny by opposing teams.

Playbooks are serious items on an NFL team. You can be fined severely for losing yours, and you can receive reprimands if you show up at the wrong meeting without it. It is, in a sense, our team bible. It contains all the essential information we need to know as we play our games. Rules. Plays. Strategies. Philosophies. Guidelines. They're all in there, and we'd better be very familiar with its contents.

I think one of the reasons a playbook is so important to a coaching staff is that they wrote the thing. They didn't go to the NFL offices and order Playbook 23—The Green Bay Packers. No, they painstakingly crafted the playbook just how they wanted us to have it. And they're personally insulted if we treat it as anything less than special.

That should give us some clues as to how God expects us to handle the Bible. It, too, is just how He wants it. It contains the information He wants us to have. It tells us what we're to do.

As you journey through life, you'll find people who aren't quite convinced that God's Word is so special. Although no one can ever prove biblical principles or teachings wrong, there are people who try to sell God's Word short—trying to detract from its value.

But remember, no teachings have withstood the test of time like the ones in the Bible. God's teachings don't always make us happy or comfortable, but they alone can make us righteous. The Bible is still the only book that we can trust in all areas of faith and practice.

This is why, if we're the least bit serious about getting into shape spiritually, we need to get into the Word of God. Steve Farrar has said, "Men of God read the Word, stay in the Word and live the Word of God."

I find a real challenge in the first two verses of the book of Psalms. They remind us that there is a certain enjoyment that should accompany our reading it, an enjoyment that leads a person to be blessed greatly.

"Blessed is the man who does not walk in the counsel of the wicked or stand in the way of sinners or sit in the seat of mockers. But his delight is in the law of the Lord, and on his law he meditates day and night" (Psalm 1: 1–2).

Like a football player pouring over the playbook so he is ready for the season, we must pour over God's Word with the same dedication.

This takes planning. In the NFL, playbook study times are pretty much dictated. In the Christian life, we're on our own. That means you have to do some planning. One suggestion is to write this time down in your Daytimer—in effect making an appointment with God.

Next, plan a place where the environment is conducive to study and meditation. Make a list of what you want to accomplish—including memorizing verses, praying for requests, and writing down your observations from the Word. I find that a prayer journal is an excellent tool.

When I asked my friend Tunch Ilkin to talk with me about the Bible, he was eager to explain the difference this Book has made in his life.

"It's made God very real to me, and it keeps reminding me of the wonderful attributes of God. It also tells me how best to live my life. I memorize and meditate on Scripture so that when tough times come, it's always there—in my head, in my mind, in my heart.

"It's simple, but not easy," he added.

"In the Psalms," Tunch continued, "David praises God continually. As Christians, we are believer-priests, and one of the jobs of the priest is to minister to God. In Old Testament times, they had the sacrifices and burnt offerings. Our sacrifices are of praise, of prayer, or of tithing."

Once we've established the habit of reading the Bible in our life, we will, if we're serious about role model responsibilities, begin to pass on that habit to our children.

There are many ways this can be done, but I like what Bryce Paup's pop did in their family.

"He would get me up every morning about 5:30 and read the Bible to me and make me learn Scripture verses. I really respected him for that. Even if I had friends over, he'd do the same thing. For a while it was embarrassing, but then I decided I was committed to this—it was what I believed. Then it didn't bother me.

"Even when I'd come home from college he'd do that. When I came back from college, I wanted to sleep in. There's a lot of late-night studying at school, and you want to do your own thing. I didn't really care for it for a while, but I had to respect his commitment to it."

What an example Bryce's dad set for his children. Remember, it takes both commitment and courage to rouse kids out of bed at 5:30 A.M. to read the Bible. And keep in mind that Bryce is six-foot five-inchs tall and weighs about 250 pounds. How'd you like to wake him up before dawn?

Being a man of God as a husband and a father is not "parenting by the seat of your pants," although it sometimes feels that way. Rather it's having a set of principals to help guide you. If you keep the playbook closed, you won't know what those principles are.

KEEP IN CONTACT WITH THE COACH

You can tell a lot about a player by how he interacts with the coach. A player who argues with the coach over his decisions and then pouts at the far corner of the bench is clearly someone you don't want your daughter dating.

On the other hand, a player who listens to the coach, tries to do what he's told, and keeps the lines of communication open is a bonus for any team. An athlete like that picks up everyone's spirits, and this makes it much easier for the coach.

Likewise, you can tell a lot about a father by how he interacts with God.

A father who doesn't talk to God must be overly self-sufficient—thinking he can take care of his family alone.

A father who doesn't talk to God is not very thankful—never taking the time to thank the Source for all his blessings.

A father who doesn't talk to God can't believe in God's love to any great extent—missing the chance to respond in kind.

A father who doesn't talk to God doesn't care much for other people—neglecting the chance to ask God to help them.

A father who doesn't talk to God is not fulfilling his job as role model for his children.

The discipline of prayer is not only vital to spiritual fitness, it's a fantastic family bonding activity. There's nothing as great as having prayer time with your wife to focus on your marriage, your family, and your kids. It's a testimony to her of your love.

The same is true with your children. As they hear you pray, you are demonstrating a prayer language that they need to become familiar with. The way you pray and see God may become the way they pray and see God.

Also, your prayers in front of the family show them that you're thankful for God's blessings. When you ask God's direction for stewardship of your resources, you remind your family that all of life's possessions come from God.

A father in prayer may be one of America's greatest needs.

But our primary purpose is not to demonstrate prayer for our families, as important as that is. The main goal is our own transformation. C.S. Lewis has said so appropriately that we start out by praying to God for something, and we find out that God changes us.

The more we pray, the more changing God will do in our hearts and the better He can guide us.

Let's see how that works for a pro football player named Mark Schlereth, a fellow offensive lineman. "Raising children is a tough responsibility," he says. "I can't imagine making all the decisions I need to without being able to pray and without having spiritual guidance.

"I think when you're raising a family, being under the authority of God means that when you do make decisions, you've prayed about them, you've thought about your actions, you've thought about the consequences of your actions. I think prayer really leads to good decisions and is a great fathering tool. "

Running back Bob Christian faced a different kind of challenge after the 1994 season ended. He got the NFL equivalent of a transfer when he was picked up by the Carolina Cougars in the expansion draft.

"My roots are kind of sunk here in Chicago," Bob said. "I've been living with my brother and I've met so many people here that I didn't really want to leave—even if it was for more money and more playing time.

When it came right down to it, I felt like I wanted to stay. When Carolina picked me, I was kind of in shock.

"The night after the draft, as I was praying, I felt the closest to God I'd felt in a long time. I was kind of opening up my heart, and He gave me kind of a sense of hope and excitement. He showed me He had great things planned for me, and that I can trust Him. He's going to be with me. It's kind of like a fresh start, not only in football but spiritually.

"To be honest, I struggle with prayer. I'm not a very good prayer. But it's important to me. ...I want to make Him Lord. If He's really my Lord, I do whatever He wants. It's not the big things, like God saying go to Africa, and I don't want to go to Africa. It's like little things, like, I probably shouldn't be flipping through this magazine instead of reading my Bible."

Before the 1995 football season, Charles Mann announced his retirement from football. But the big guy who won Super Bowl rings for both Washington and San Francisco is not about to retire from his main job—as father and husband. And he sounds like he's eager to make sure he's as successful as a praying dad as he was a football player.

"I pray over my children," says the main Mann. "I let them openly hear me ask for blessings from the Lord for them. I pray over my daughter. I put my hand on her as we're praying, and I say, 'Lord, bless Camille.' I pray that she will be a strong woman of God, and I just let her hear me asking the Lord for these blessings on her life.

"...I go through a similar prayer with my son, who is three. And I pray over my baby. ...I think the power comes from them hearing my concern."

If you need to see how it can work in your house, here's how it happens around Charles Mann's home. "I put the kids to bed, so I'm in there praying every day. I win that contest! I keep trying to spend some quiet family time, say from about 7:00 to 7:30 every night, where we go through the Word. Satan wants to make sure we're not consistent, so he'll throw in a dilemma. He'll keep you busy.

"My pastor once told me, 'Look, I'm tired of hearing this about not having enough time in the day. We all have the same amount of time. It's what you prioritize in your life.'"

FIND WORKOUT PARTNERS

Spiritual growth is not a solo act. Oh, we may pray alone at times, and we need to get alone with God and His Word. But we can't look through the New Testament and miss the fact that God designed Christians to be part of a unit.

Even in prison, Paul worshipped with Silas in what may have been the first small group meeting. Seriously, you can't run the risk as dads of trying to do this alone. We all need the help of mentors, accountability partners, teachers, or prayer partners.

And think of the example we set for our children when we join hands spiritually with other men. They can see the unity, the sense of community, and the multiplied importance of spiritual disciplines.

Small accountability groups are a great asset. When you form a small group, make commitments to each other promising to honor, support, and strengthen one another through the struggles, temptations, and responsibilities of life.

Your goal is to challenge one another to excellence. Help each other out when you're weak, but also ignite each other to action. Receive the wisdom and counsel of others. Proverbs 15:22 says, "Plans fail for lack of counsel, but with many advisors, they succeed."

One great benefit is being continually renewed through the support of other's prayers. James 5:16 says, "Therefore confess your sins to each other and pray for each other so that you may be healed. The prayer of a righteous man is powerful and effective."

Finally, small groups are fun. You get to enjoy the richness and flavor of laughter shared with others who are in Christ. Differences can be enjoyed—and yet it's encouraging to realize you're all facing similar battles.

To start a small group, pray for God to show you and others how to get a group of men together. Make the invitations personal. Encourage men to come. Let them know there will be a strong commitment to honor confidentiality within the group.

It's beneficial to have either Bible study or other Christian books or tapes to use as resources. You should also have a stated period of time and purpose. Men don't want to sign up for something with no end in sight.

Aside from a small group, another possibility for teaming up is a ministry project, either at church or in the community. These can provide some great growing and bonding times for men.

Matt Millen also values small group accountability. "I still have to fight not doing things by myself. I go to a Bible study, I have some accountability there and with my wife. But still, it's hard for me to find somebody who is strong enough and wouldn't be afraid to say to me, 'Man, you're a jerk.'

"I don't have that.

"Leo was good for me. With Wizz, he'd say, 'Man, who're you kidding with this? You're not doing it for that, you're doing it for this.' I loved it. Finally, somebody was telling me something."

In addition to small group involvement, we men who are setting the pattern for our children need to have a church where we can worship, learn, lead, and work. Anthony Muñoz talks about how important that was in his spiritual life when he first went to the Bengals.

"You really look at what's important in life. For us, it was getting plugged into a church right away here in Cincinnati. Early in our growth, God put us around some really good Bible teachers and well-balanced churches so we were also able to see the importance of small group Bible studies at home.

"If you get away from studying or you get away from getting together with other believers, you don't feel as energized, you don't feel as confident as you go through every day."

It's true. We lose strength when we lose relationships.

Did you know that the average life of a player in the NFL is less than five years?

I feel fortunate that I've been able to stick around for more than ten years. But I didn't gain this longevity by training only during the season—or by going it alone. I train as a way of life, year-round. Your approach to working out with God should be the same.

PERSONAL TIME-OUT

1. In what ways am I a "soft" Christian? If people were rating Christians by what they saw in me, how might I imply Christians were wimps? What spiritual activities would beef me up for the Lord?

2. How strong is my commitment to God? Would I be a first round draft pick, a free agent, or someone who would be overlooked completely if a draft of Christians were held? How much progress have I made in my workouts with God in the past six months? What goals should I set for the next six months?

3. Is my relationship with God right now warm, cold, hot, or indifferent?

4. How often do I read the Bible in a week? What is the last biblical truth that I dug out of the Scriptures myself? How can I set up a Bible reading time? A schedule? Should I also set up a time to read with my children and wife?

5. When I talk to God, do I have faith that He recognizes my voice? That He is good? How can I better pray for my children? In their presence?

RUETTGERS' REFLECTIONS

Football truths that also work in real life

Ninety percent of the game is mental.

Balance is one of the most important keys.

Focus!

It's a long season. A lot will happen between now and the end.

CHAPTER EIGHT

Exercising Your Character

My father is my role model because he is a very respectable, hard-working man. He doesn't have a problem with anyone. Everyone likes him. Even little kids love him.

—A TEENAGER

Former UCLA basketball coach John Wooden was the kind of person we can all admire as not just a coach but a great role model. His life was an open book that his players, fans, and observers could read freely. And central to the plot of his life was his desire to have godly character.

"Be more concerned with your character than with your reputation," Coach Wooden said, "because your character is what you really are, while your reputation is merely what others think you are."[1]

Your character is what you really are. Think of the ramifications of that statement. It echoes the remark of Bill Brooks of the Buffalo Bills, who told me, "Football is what I do, not who I am."

Amazingly enough, some people don't see good character as an issue with our leadership today. Take this response from a young person to a *USA Today* "Voices Across The USA" question posing whether sexual harassment charges leveled at President Clinton were relevant to his job performance:

"I don't think it is relevant. It shouldn't make a difference in his job."

I noted that the young woman who answered that way lives here in Green Bay. There's a growing number of people who are willing to overlook character flaws and concentrate solely on a person's job performance.

Let's hope they're not fathers—who are all in high places.

HIGH STANDARDS FOR HIGH PLACES

There is a certain amount of celebrity status that comes from being a professional football player in the National Football League. It's enabled me to meet pro athletes from other sports as well as some of Hollywood's noted celebrities. Believe me, it's interesting to meet and get to know some of the more famous people of our time.

A few years ago my interests turned from silver screen stars to politicians and leaders. I suppose doing a campaign appearance for then Vice President George Bush and meeting Lee Iococca piqued my interests. Communicating with Rush Limbaugh and with state and local political leaders has became somewhat of a hobby.

A couple years ago, I became familiar with a couple of political leaders and their families. They carried serious clout. They made the laws and enforced them in their land. Obviously, they weren't American politicians. They were foreign leaders from overseas. Powerful, rich, and influential throughout their nation.

What I found most interesting was their family life. It was rotten. They were so consumed by their responsibilities of state that they forgot about their homes. Many of their children turned out to be rebellious.

One politician's son raped his half-sister. Another son murdered his half-brother. And one son formed an army and tried to overthrow his own father in a military coup. Although he was prince in the lineage of his father, this son was known by the people as a man of shameful things.

Their names, if you haven't already guessed, are Eli and Samuel, judges of the nation of Israel, and King Saul, King David, and King Solomon. These were some of the mightiest rulers of Israel in the Old Testament.

Eli was a godly man who became a judge for the nation of Israel. He was so busy leading his people that he overlooked teaching his sons about character. His sons "were wicked men with no regard for the Lord." They later became so rebellious that Eli had no authority over them, leading to their demise.

Samuel, under the tutelage of Eli, became the next judge and was also a great, godly leader for Israel. But the people grew tired of a judge and wanted a king, as their neighboring nations had. They cited Samuel's age and the fact that his sons, appointed as the new leaders, were corrupt.

"They turned aside after dishonest gain and accepted bribes and perverted justice" (1 Samuel 8:3).

Those are sad stories of men who did not pass on character to their children. As men of God who want to do better than that, our goal should be three-fold in regard to character: First, we must be men of high character. Second, we must display virtuous character traits. Third, we've got to aim high—as Jimmy Stewart made clear when he read these comments at a Super Bowl effort to promote drug-free living:

- A good role model knows what he believes and he practices it no matter what the consequences. He's willing to sacrifice his time to make his values come alive.
- Role models aren't just talk; their walk bears out who and what they are.
- Role models are never too big to serve others, and they never begin to think that they're so smart that they don't need teaching themselves.
- A good role model can show strength or gentleness, and he knows which one to use when it is needed.
- A good role model always play by the rules.
- A good role model is willing to share his gifts with others.
- A good role model never becomes so used to succeeding that he can't remember what it feels like to fail.[2]

That, my friend, is a tall order, a high hurdle. But we must remember that we have a power source to accomplish this daunting goal. The Holy Spirit living within us can guide us toward improvement where it's needed.

Writer Gordon H. Taggart aims high as well: "I wish I were honest enough to admit all my shortcomings, brilliant enough to accept flattery without it making me arrogant, tall enough to tower above deceit, strong enough to treasure love, brave enough to welcome criticism, compassionate enough to understand human frailties, wise enough to recognize my mistakes, humble enough to appreciate greatness, staunch enough to stand firm by my friends, human enough to be thoughtful of my neighbor, and righteous enough to be devoted to the love of God."

Without the Holy Spirit's help, those *would* just be wishes—pipe dreams of a frustrated role model wanna-be. But with the assistance of God's Holy Spirit, you can be the kind of man you hope to be. Not perfect, mind you, but progressing toward improvement.

"Talent is God-given. Be humble. Fame is man-given. Be thankful. Conceit is self-given. Be careful."

JOHN WOODEN
FORMER COACH
UCLA BRUINS

While we usually think of each other in terms of our career paths, we must remember that our occupation is a means of making a living, not the mark of our existence.

I may be a football player, but who I am is more complicated. Who I am is the sum of my actions, my words, my relationships, and my impact on my world. And nothing can summarize who I am better than my character.

As we get more specific about individual character qualities that we should be exercising, it's not easy to pick out just a few. But those I've chosen to focus on can truly make us better dads and more effective role models.

HUMILITY

While Coach Wooden's contributions are still fresh in our minds, I'd like to cite another one. Wooden, in addition to his great coaching prowess, was a humble champion. We don't often see those two words right next to each other, do we? Instead, we've grown accustomed to champions who wag their index finger, strut their stuff, and pose for the camera.

Coach Wooden seemed almost embarrassed by the adulation his ten national championships gave him. That's why I know he meant every word of a sign that, according to *They Call Me Coach,* hangs in the locker room at County Stadium in Milwaukee: Talent is God-given. Be humble. Fame is man-given. Be thankful. Conceit is self-given. Be careful.

Humble leadership is hard to challenge. Sure, there'll be people who try to walk all over a man who demonstrates humility, but if he also has other traits mentioned later in this chapter, they won't get far.

What men like that don't understand is that our egos can be our biggest stumbling blocks. Ego can be our biggest adversary in our drive to be the man God wants us to be.

In 1991 we had some ego problems on our offensive line. The offensive line is generally the group that has the best quality guys. We know we're not going to get any attention anyway, so we just go out and work, sweat, and grind.

But for whatever reason, that year our offensive line had real problems. The main cause was big egos. That was the year the NFL salary scale skyrocketed. Every guy was looking at the other guy wondering if he was worth the money he was getting paid. Instead of focusing on teamwork and playing in the same direction, we were playing in opposite directions.

We had four guys in that group who were all first-rounders. None of us could put our egos on the back burner long enough to benefit the team and work on the goals. That was not only one of the worst seasons for the Packers in recent history, but it was also one of the worst years for me.

I have to admit that I was part of the problem. Offensive linemen need to work together. A lot of times an offensive line's strength isn't in the individuals, it's in the synergy that is created by the whole sum. Our egos wouldn't let us achieve that synergy.

The real problem, though, is not that egos sometimes make for bad football teams, but that high egos make for bad families.

I remember one point in my life when I had little humility and a lot of ego. I came home from work one afternoon and my wife told me that she needed me to do something for her. When I refused, Sheryl said, "Ken, the world doesn't revolve around you!"

My response was, "It most certainly does!"

I'm not proud of that response. Things have changed so much since then—I can't believe I ever said anything like that! But my ego was destroying my marriage.

At the professional level, athletes are so pampered and we focus so completely on one thing—helping our team win—we sometimes fall into being egocentric. And at any level, whether we play a sport or not, it may seem difficult to stoop to the level of humility we need to be to be an effective role model.

My buddy Tunch Ilkin told me a great story about his former owner when he played for Pittsburgh. His name is Art Rooney, and I think what he did one day at the ballpark can challenge us to keep the ego where it belongs.

"Art Rooney was the owner of the Pittsburgh Steelers. He was probably the patriarch in the NFL. If anyone had a reason to be all swelled up with himself, it was the chief. Everyone would affectionately call Art Rooney the 'Chief.'

"...He was just a regular guy from the Northside of Pittsburgh. When he grew up, Northside was a typical working-class neighborhood, and it's pretty much the same now. It's the inner city. He never left that neighborhood. Even when he had tons of money, he still lived on the Northside.

"One of the things he always did was to make everyone feel like they were the big shot and that he was just this city kid from the Northside.

"I remember every time he'd see me at the locker, he'd say, 'Tunch, my boy, are they still killing each other over there?' speaking of my homeland, where there was civil war.

"When I was in the hospital in traction, with my back all messed up, he brought me cookies.

"Before the draft in 1980, I was brought into Pittsburgh for a physical, and so was a guy named Nate Johnson, a wide receiver from some small college. We'd just got done seeing the doctor, and we were waiting for whatever was next.

"As we're sitting there, Mr. Rooney walks in, dressed very casual. He began cleaning the ash trays out in the lobby. Nate looks at him and says, 'So, Buddy, what are you, the janitor?'

"Well, I knew who it was, so I'm appalled and embarrassed for Nate. My face is red, my ears were burning. But the Chief just played it out. He

HALFTIME POINTERS

The Measure of a Guy—a Self-Test

➢ Am I a kind kind of guy? When I drive the car? When I mention others not present? When I face a relationship problem? When I disagree with someone? When I watch sports? When I play sports? When I have an over-eager salesman in a bad suit at my door (yikes!)?

➢ Do I know what I've got? Take a closer look at the list of character qualities discussed in this chapter. Mark a paper with four columns: Stunningly Strong, Remarkably So-So, Embarassingly Weak, Disgustingly Absent. Now place each character quality in the appropriate columns for you. Dare to ask your wife if she agrees with your assessments. Clue: if she laughs a lot, you probably have some homework.

➢ Honest to Goodness. Take ten big points on the tote board for every time you:

- Report the right figures on your income tax.
- Give back overcharges at the store.
- Drive the speed limit.
- Work the required amount of time.
- Pay for your personal calls.

said, 'Oh, I do a little bit of everything around here. I clean up, whatever needs to be done, I do it. Rooney's the name.'

"And that was all. That was just so typical of the way the Chief was. He was just such a regular guy. I don't know how he stood spiritually, but I tell you what, he lived his life like Jesus told us to."

COMPASSION

I suppose it seems a bit odd for a football player to be talking about the importance of compassion. After all, if you see us during the three hours a week when we are playing our game, we don't seem like very kind people.

But you have to remember that this is our job—not who we are. We may pound an opponent relentlessly all day, but he's ready for the pounding. He knows what he is getting into, so it's not a matter of my not being nice to a defender—I won't let him get to our quarterback.

In fact, the NFL is full of genuinely kind and compassionate people.

As you may recall, there are three levels of role model influence. But sometimes we're kind and compassionate to people in our family—while we fail to extend ourselves beyond that sphere.

You may be challenged by the following story, told by a writer named Peggy Ellsberg.

"Soon after I got married, I met, by chance, a young couple with lots of children.

"Jim and Mary had recently moved into a small, four-room flat near the church. Jim struck up a conversation with my husband in a bookstore and invited us to lunch the next day after Sunday mass.

"As planned, we waited until Jim and Mary and their children filed out of church, and as we all stood chatting on the steps, Jim also invited Don, a law student who was standing there alone. Then he invited a young couple who spoke almost no English.

"As we all proceeded toward the apartment, Mary spotted their elderly neighbor out walking her dog. She came to lunch, too.

"Jim and Mary had almost no money, but they invited all sorts of people in to eat with them every Sunday. The menu consisted of boiled spaghetti with canned tomato sauce. On some Sundays, there were twenty people crowded around the table. I remember those simple plates of spaghetti as some of the most delicious meals I've ever eaten. Spiced with the simplicity of the Gospel."[3]

Now there's an example of kindness and compassion in action—and appreciated!

FAITH

This is so fundamental, so basic, yet so important. It's a little like the story about Vince Lombardi, the great Packer coach of an earlier generation. Supposedly, he called the team together for the first meeting, held up a pigskin for the whole team to see, and bellowed, "Gentlemen, this is a football."

I can imagine there were some rookies who wanted to raise their hands and ask Coach to slow down a little.

We all need constant reminders that our faith is the cornerstone of our life. We need faith to believe that our fathering by God's standards is going to work. We need faith that when God's appointed dads to be the authority figure in the home, he would also help us with directions.

Any time a football team shows up for camp and begins to study the coach's scheme for the year, he has to have faith that if he and his teammates carry out the designs of the coach, they'll be successful. Likewise, we have to believe that God's guidelines for our families will bring success as well.

Look at a father like Abraham of the Old Testament. He had to have incredible faith to take his son Isaac with him on a journey that he thought would end with Isaac being slain as a sacrifice. How many of us would even consider such a journey?

But think of the object lesson that was for Isaac when he saw how much faith Abraham had in God.

Garth Jax of the Phoenix Cardinals talked with me about the importance of being grounded in faith. "It's important for anybody, especially a role model, to be grounded in the Christian faith. That's why I want my child, first of all, to be grounded in the Word. And second, I want his or her role model to have the same beliefs, the same morals."

INTEGRITY

I'd like to tell a story about Theodore Roosevelt. It's told he was once riding with a couple of his cowboys, and they lassoed a steer.

They brought the cow down to the ground, lit a fire, and prepared to apply a brand. They just so happened to be on Roosevelt's neighbor, Greg Lang's land. And the rule of the day was that if you lassoed a steer and branded it, it belonged to the man whose land you were on.

As one of Roosevelt's cattle boys applied the brand to the cow, Roosevelt said, "Wait! It should be Lang's brand."

"That's all right, boss," said the cattle boy.

"But you're putting on my brand," Roosevelt protested.

"That's right," said the man.

"Drop that iron!" Roosevelt demanded, "Get back to the ranch and get out. I don't need you anymore. A man who will steal for me, will steal from me."[4]

Although that happened close to one hundred years ago, it doesn't mean that integrity is so old-fashioned it's not good anymore. Now, more than ever, our world is suffering an integrity crisis. We simply don't know who to believe anymore.

Yet integrity is so simple. It's a characteristic as easy as telling the truth, keeping our word, and being honest. I like the calm and easy way Herschel Walker described his own striving for integrity.

"I do what's right," said Herschel. "It's funny, if you're always running away from something, if you're a criminal inside, you're not happy because you're always looking over your back. But when you have peace of mind, you're able to go to sleep at night without keeping with one eye open. You're confident.

"I think that's the key. Do what's right. And it's not that hard to do what's right. It's harder to frown than it is to smile."

Even when it might seem hard to have integrity, that's when a valued role model can step in and simplify matters. Eugene Robinson of the Seattle Seahawks related how teammate Dave Brown did that for him.

"I look up to Dave Brown," began Eugene. "He discipled me when I first came on the Seahawks.

"And he reminded me the other day how important it is to make sure my word is my bond. He told me I gave my word to him, and I didn't follow through.

"I said, 'Man, what are you talking about?'

"He said, 'A simple thing. You said you were going to cut my hair, and you didn't cut it. I looked for you the next day, and you had forgotten your clippers, and then you looked like you were avoiding me. I made plans for you to do it. You gave your word, and your word is your bond.'

"I thought of all the areas of my life where I gave my word, and I failed.

"Then he said, 'Gene, if you're not faithful in the small things, how are you going to be faithful in the big things?'"

That's how a role model can make a difference in a person's life when integrity is the issue.

CONSISTENCY

An article in Parade magazine asked young people what they hate to hear from their parents. One sixteen-year-old said she despised the phrase, "When I was your age." To her, it was hypocritical.

"My parents will tell me stories about how they would cut school and go to the beach, but then they're like 'If we ever catch you doing that....' Or they'll reminisce about how they threw water balloons at their principal. ...But now he's like 'if I ever catch you doing anything like that...' "[5]

I see hypocrisy in the pro sports field more often than I would like. There are always one or two guys who step forward minutes before the start of a game and proclaim an immediate need for commitment and sacrifice. Often these guys are nowhere to be found during the week's preparation.

You never see them in the weight room pumping iron. You never see them spending extra time in the film room studying their opponents. They don't even notice that their words don't quite align with their actions. They feel they're giving it their all. But ask their teammates. They know that our actions in preparation speak louder than our pre-game words of dedication.

I was watching Oprah Winfrey one day, and a prominent politician's wife was on. Toward the end of the show, she told a story about how her father would always say, "Do as I say, not as I do." First Oprah's guest joked about how ridiculous that sounded, but then she said, "What we need to bring back today is a little bit of that hypocrisy."

I couldn't believe my ears. Was she confused? After a minute I realized she was dead serious.

Think about it: is there anything more damaging to a child than a parent who can't be trusted? A parent-child relationship is a tightrope walk most of the time anyway. And a lifestyle of inconsistencies from mom or dad is bound to knock a child off balance.

COMMITMENT

I'm big on commitment—could be why I've been with one football team for more than ten years. The team has honored its commitment to me, and I want to make sure I honor my commitment to the team.

Of course, commitment isn't easy, and it sure isn't popular with everyone. We can see it in the divorce rate. We can see it in the corporate world, where companies move away from their employees or where employees leave their company, always looking for a better deal. We can see it in Christians, who are committed to their worship community only as long as they get what they want out of their church.

I love a scene from the movie *A Bronx Tale*. Robert DeNiro plays the father of a boy who is seeking a role model in the Bronx's inner-city neighborhood in the 1960s. His boy gets hooked up with a gangster and begins working for him as a runner and gofer.

The father, a bus driver, pulls the son aside and asks him if he thinks the mobster is a tough guy. "I'll tell you what tough is. Tough is getting up every morning and going to work, doing the same job, driving that bus every morning."

It probably can't be said better than that.

Matt Stover tells a great story, too. His dad instilled commitment in him—the hard way.

"We sold programs at Cowboys games. It didn't matter how cold or hot it was or how much it was raining. You didn't back out just because you didn't like the situation. My dad would say, 'You're going.' And I would go out there and freeze at the Cotton Bowl games or in the parking lot at a Cowboy game.

"Those parking lots get windy. It's twenty degrees out there, and here you are, a ten-year-old kid. I remember bawling my head off because I was miserable and my dad was making me stand out there and sell his programs—even though they weren't selling.

"But what it taught me was commitment. You have to be committed to what you're setting out to do. You can't quit. That's not what it's about. I wouldn't have learned that unless my dad had forced me to do that."

CONVICTION

In 1994, I was offered the opportunity to do a United Way spot as a representative of the Green Bay Packers. Anyone who watches Monday Night Football assumes that the spokesperson for the United Way is a good player and a good role model. So when our public relations director first described the opportunity, I wanted to jump at the chance.

Then I heard that the United Way supported Planned Parenthood. I told my PR guy that I'd have to get back to him. I went home and sought some wise counsel, thought about it, and prayed about it. Finally, I decided to turn down the opportunity.

When the Packer PR department asked me why I turned it down, I wrote a letter giving my reasons, based on the Bible, why I couldn't support an organization which sponsors abortions.

I think the Bible clearly tells us that human life is a blessing from God to be cherished and protected.

Having convictions—caring about the right causes—is part of building character. But standing up for one's convictions takes courage and a thick skin, as the following story from my life points out.

Retired New York Giant offensive lineman and Super Bowl champion Chris Godfrey and I had been invited to share an alternative view to abortion at a public high school in Menasha, Wisconsin.

However, as the date approached, the engagement was canceled because of threats made by people who opposed our visit. The town went up in arms over the controversy created by the issue.

The town's paper, the *Appleton Post Crescent,* was flooded by letters to the editor, and they came gushing out in the opinion section for many days.

Two weeks later, we were invited by a private school down the street to come in for the same purpose. When we arrived, we saw news cameras, reporters, and a man who opposed our views sitting in the second row of the students, recording our every word.

The discussion went well. We reminded the students to make their own intelligent decisions—after they were well-informed about both sides of the issue. After we finished, Chris and I signed autographs and visited personally with the students, who were very receptive.

After an article about our visit appeared in the *Appleton Post Crescent*, the paper was again flooded by letters to the opinion section.

Then one of the paper's sports reporters got into the act. Here's what he wrote:

"Ken Ruettgers, that rascal, is at it again. The Green Bay Packers' left tackle, who is more well-known for his training camp holdouts than anything he's ever done on the field, was in Menasha Wednesday night as a member of a group called Pro-Life Athletes.

"He was speaking to the kids about abortion and why his group is opposed to it. The kids sat in rapt attention as Ruettgers, and others, spoke on a subject they know nothing about.

"'I grew up believing that abortion is morally wrong,' he told the group. 'I guess my point is that a lot of people know what the truth is.'

"Surely they do.

"The truth is, Ruettgers and his cronies should probably butt out of such issues and pay more attention to what they're being handsomely overpaid to do."

It was all so weird. I never could have predicted the mammoth commotion created by our visit. We'd been invited to share our opinions—the same opinions held and taught by the school we visited—about the sacredness of life.

Other editorials soon appeared in the paper in response to this article. Most were positive and appreciative of our efforts and time. I was pleasantly surprised to see my teammates rally to my support in the form of a letter to the editor.

But the sports reporter-turned-cornerback intercepted their letter. He used it to build his second article about our seemingly harmless visit to a private school. This piece of journalism was titled "Packers Should Abort Letter-writing Campaign." It read:

"Let's file this one under, 'Gee don't you guys have anything better to do?'"

We certainly didn't.

The controversy continued for some time, and letters to the editor in support of our convictions poured in. Every one of those letters meant a lot.

Too often these days, when you stand up for values and morals in our politically correct society, you'll be told that you don't know what you're talking about. The politically correct critic will tell you, "Let the experts handle it. They know more than you do."

Sometimes this is true. But one of the greatest gifts we have in America is the ability to form convictions, make our own educated decisions, voice our opinions, and carry out our dreams and desires.

Once you're convicted about what is right, don't let anyone knock you over.

You don't have to be a professional athlete to write an articulate letter to the editor. In fact if you're not a football player you may have a better chance to write a well-punctuated letter!

There was one thing this sports writer forgot to let his readers know about my teammates and their letter backing me up. They signed off with, "Standing for something." Below that were their names.

That's more than any critic has ever said.

PERSONAL TIME-OUT

1. Where do I stand on the character question?
Do I think people in leadership positions should be held accountable for their character? How important is character where I work?

2. Humility is slippery. How can I know if I have it, without being proud of it?

3. Would my children consider me compassionate?
What have I done in the past week out of kindness alone?

4. What do I do each day to solidify my faith? How can I pass it along to my children or people I have contact with each day? How can I impact someone outside my first and second spheres of influence?

5. If someone were checking my integrity, which area of my life would I not want him to investigate? How can I change this?

6. How can I demonstrate my conviction about a cause? Have I ever written a letter to the editor?

RUETTGERS' REFLECTIONS

Football truths that also work in real life

If you lose your composure in the battle, you'll lose the war.

Give 100 percent—100 percent of the time.

If you cheat yourself, you cheat the team.

CHAPTER NINE

Love-Training for Marriage

My mom is my role model because she wants the best for me. I want to be like my mom when I grow up. She tells me about her teenage years. She hopes for me to finish school and go to college just as she did

—TEENAGE GIRL

It's far too early to tell if my son, Matthew, will become a football player like his daddy, but one thing I know. If he does, a big reason will be that he's been immersed in the game so deeply—and he wants to follow his dad's lead.

In baseball, Ken Griffey Jr. is a prime example of a boy who learned the game from watching his daddy play. During one season, veteran Ken Griffey and teenage son Ken Jr. were teammates for the Seattle Mariners. Imagine the levels of role modeling going on in that situation!

Junior Griffey began to learn the game as a kid when his dad was a part of Cincinnati's Big Red Machine in the early seventies. He had the rare opportunity of hanging around one of the best teams ever assembled and observing close-up such greats as Pete Rose, Tony Perez, Johnny Bench, and, of course, his dad.

Among the other rug rats who were scurrying around the Riverfront Astroturf were Pete Rose Jr., Eduardo Perez, and Pedro Borbon. All four of these children of the Reds grew up to be just like daddy—they played professional baseball.

Time will tell if Matthew becomes a player—or even wants to become one. But every time I play, he needs look no further than big number 75 to find a football role model. Of course, if he decides to be a quarterback, he'll need to look elsewhere, but why wouldn't he want to be one of football's unsung heroes?

And yet, there's a lot more important matters in the Ruettgers household than how Dad plays football. Matt, Katherine, and Susan are watching Sheryl and me every day to see how well we're doing in a much more important institution than the NFL. They see us demonstrate marriage every day.

I can't even estimate what a vital responsibility this is! As each day passes around the Ruettgers household, I'm aware that as my children observe me, they learn valuable lessons about marriage—and especially how a husband should treat his wife.

Can our society have any bigger need than this? If we have any hope of redeeming this culture, we dads must take the lead by showing our children the right way to be a husband and father. We must demonstrate love for their mother in such an impressive way that our children find it irresistible.

When we do, our sons will learn how to treat girls in general and their future wife in particular. Our daughters will know they don't have to look at anyone but Dad to find a model for who they should marry. And our world will grow stronger, one new family at a time.

Strong families are basic building blocks for a strong society. It's no mystery why God established marriage and the family as the first societal institution (Genesis 2). He was constructing the foundation for all cultures that would develop.

And notice that in Noah's day, when society failed because of sin and had to be reestablished, God again used the family as the foundation (Genesis 6-8).

Please understand that in holding up the ideal, I'm not suggesting that those of us in two-parent homes are better people or Christians than moms and dads who have seen their marriages disintegrate. On the contrary, I recognize that I'm just as capable as destroying a marriage as the next person.

What I do want to suggest is that we value what we have and make every effort to preserve it. And if you're not living in an intact marriage, your responsibility to model the Christian life is no less important. In fact,

I would guess that your job is tougher than mine.

Being the right kind of husband and dad is a tough job, no matter what our situation. Sometimes I think we lose sight of the power we have to either destroy or nurture our marriages. Like other areas, we need training. In this case, love training. This power, thank goodness, is to be shared with your wife.

So how can you be the best husband you're capable of?

Such a vast but sacred undertaking must be broke down into smaller steps. Sometimes you gain the most yards on the ground, one great run at a time.

FOUR DOWNS OF LOVE TRAINING

THE FIRST DOWN:
A HUNK OF METAL—OR YOUR WIFE?

Think of the things guys treasure. Like cars. Let's say a guy gets a Jeep Cherokee. It's a good-looking machine, and the owner is understandably proud of it. He treats it like a rare museum piece. He protects it from the sun's nasty rays. He talks about it to his friends. He never says a disparaging word about it—or tolerates any criticism from his buddies.

It seems silly to even make the comparison, but sometimes we treasure our wives less than we treasure some hunk of metal with four-wheel drive. Recall the words of Jesus, "Where your treasure is, there your heart will be also" (Matthew 6:21).

I wonder what our kids learn from us when they see us treasure things more than people? And recreation more than spiritual health?

Bill Hybels, pastor of Willow Creek Church in the Chicago area, said, "If you let me hang around you long enough, I could determine what you really treasure in life. Even if you tried to fool, sidetrack, or mislead me, the truth about your treasure will eventually show up. But what you treasure shows up in your conversation and schedules, your close friends and spending habits."[1]

Hybels then pointed to an interesting phenomenon that follows the courtship stage of a male-female relationship. "Then came the wedding, the honeymoon, and the move into the apartment. At this point married men do something completely instinctive. They shift their attention to the next goal in life, to succeed in a career. Most newly married men aren't aware of this shift, but it transforms their lives."

He's right. In fact, I found myself making a similar leap soon after Sheryl and I were married.

Hybels went on to say, "When a boy shifts to sports, he learns how the game works. First the tryouts, then the practices, the games, the tournaments, and then the award banquets. Then he puts away the uniform, waits about three weeks, and shifts his focus to the next sport."

"My wife has brought out of me things I didn't know were in me. God put the right woman in my life."

REGGIE WHITE
GREEN BAY PACKERS

Because we know we're vulnerable to this kind of thinking, we men should take steps to keep our focus on the right things. One way to do that is to make this verse our motto: "Husbands, love your wives" (Ephesians 5:25).

That seems like such a simple command, but consider this: There's no command in the Bible that says, "Wives, love your husbands." We men have a tendency to let the mundane things in life interfere with our love. We have to be reminded to act out our love, to show our wives we treasure them—much more than a hunk of metal or a fishing pole.

Herschel and Cindy Walker have been married twelve years. Listen to the great running back talk about his favorite girl:

"We're so compatible. What I like, she likes. We've known each for sixteen years, and we went to college together. She's from New York, and I'm from Georgia. But we love being with each other. We're the best of friends. We don't go out trying to work at our marriage, because our marriage works. We love being with each other."

Kevin Glover, 282-pound center for the Detroit Lions, speaks of his wife Cestaine, a law school graduate and the mother of their infant child: "She's the most important person on earth in my life right now, and she has been for a number of years. We met as freshmen in college and have been close ever since."

Reggie White rarely misses an opportunity to praise his wife, Sara. "She's helped me so much in my life," White said. "She's served in a lot of ways within my family. She's brought out of me things I didn't know were in me. It's helped my character. God put the right woman in my life."

Imagine the security and confidence it brings children to hear Dad say such wonderful things about their mother. They need to know that Dad's best friend is their mom. And they need to know their greatest treasure among earthly things will be the person they marry.

THE SECOND DOWN:
STAY COMMITTED—OR LOSE YOUR CONTRACT FOREVER

If we truly treasure our wife, we'll do everything to keep our marriage functioning and strong. But there's another, less romantic reason for doing so.

We promised we would.

The power of a promise kept is perhaps one of the greatest lessons we can teach our children. The current Promise Keepers movement, which challenges us to keep our vows, has drawn hundreds of thousands of men to fill football stadiums to learn better how.

Among the seven promises that Promise Keepers are asked to keep is a vow to build strong marriages and families.

That promise is nothing new. It's a vow we made on the day we were married. We stood before friends and family—and most importantly God—and committed ourselves to the woman we loved.

Keeping our marriage vows can be the challenge of a lifetime. Honoring vows and pledges is not something we can do without effort, and sometimes it'd be easier to say, "I just can't keep this promise any more."

One man who's had to work to keep his marriage commitment is Mike Horan, a kicker with Philadelphia, Denver, and the New York Giants during his ten-year NFL career. He and his wife, Kim, began a fundraising effort while Mike was with Denver, and Punts With a Purpose is still going strong.

But Mike and Kim needed help to make sure their marriage stayed strong. "Making the decision that my marriage is important and divorce isn't an option was an important step for me," Horan explained. "I needed some help, I needed some more tools.

"I grew up in a home where my father was an alcoholic and my mother was a rage-aholic. We just didn't have the best role models in helping us deal with our kids. If I'd grown up in a 'normal' family, maybe I would have learned some things differently.

"I want to make my marriage work, and I need help doing it. I could say, 'Fine, let's just split and go on.' But that doesn't solve the problem. When a person decides to opt out of a marriage, he's going to take the same patterns and programming to the next relationship.

"My wife got to the point where she said, 'Look, we need some changes.' I wouldn't say she gave me an ultimatum, but she said, 'I'm not happy the way things are, and I would rather end the relationship. If we end it now, we can remain friends for the kids' sake, but I can't continue to live with you the way things are right now.'

"We found a counselor who dealt specifically with my problem, which was anger. His name is Gary Oliver and he's made the biggest impact in my life. Kim and I have been married for twelve years. Learning to manage my anger has made the biggest difference."

Remaining committed to a marriage that was in trouble helped Mike Horan restore the relationship with his wife. And now their daughters Meghan and Shawna, and their son, Michael William II, can watch as their dad models for them how a life can be changed for God's glory.

Author Gary Smalley has some suggestions for us to follow as we seek the glue that will bond our families together without danger of a split. He wrote, "Whatever the issue or crisis, five elements will hold the family together and greatly increase the likelihood that your marriage will thrive. Healthy couples:

1. Have a clearly defined set of expectations.
2. Understand and practice meaningful communication.
3. Are associated with a small healthy support group.
4. Are aware of unhealthy or offensive behaviors stemming from the patterns they inherited from their parents.

5. Have a vibrant relationship with Jesus Christ."[2]

The goal of all this, of course, is to have a thriving marriage that encourages individual growth for each partner and a growing sense of responsibility toward each other.

That began to happen in Karl Meklenburg's life when he realized he wasn't behaving in a way that demonstrated commitment to his family.

"I got to a point where I had to rely on God," says the Denver linebacker. "Things were terrible, but He said that if I was faithful to Him, everything would work out the way he planned. I had to actually look at myself, my life, and my family, and say, 'I've been doing this all wrong. This isn't what you want, Lord. This isn't what I want.'

"All of a sudden, I stopped going hunting or fishing every day off. I started helping my wife, talking to her about what's going on at work, and what her problems are at home. What's she's feeling and what am I feeling?

"I guess I needed to be put in a situation where I didn't feel like I could fix it myself. Hard work had always been enough before. Then I realized there's a lot more to life than going to the weight room and doing all that running. That's going to help me in football, but in the long run, that's not going to help me in life.

"...I used to think if I was involved at home, I wouldn't have anything left for football. But that's not true. Not only did God want me to be a football player, he wanted me to be a good father and a good husband, and I had energy to do them all."

As husbands, we need to be into love-training, not excuse-making. Anyone can wimp out and find a reason to jump overboard when the seas get rough and the water starts coming in. To keep our marriages afloat, we need to find ways to fix the leaks, turn the sails, or head for safety.

Some may need help from a fellow sailor, as Mike Horan did. Others may need to concentrate on the task and back off on the stuff that doesn't matter, as Karl Meklenburg did.

How can you better honor the vow you made on your wedding day? Remember, your kids are watching.

THE THIRD DOWN: COMPENSATE FOR DIFERENCES—OR GET DROPPED FOR A LOSS

I think it's amusing. Here's a truth the church has known for centuries, but has lately fallen into disrepute in the secular media. Now suddenly it comes roaring back — as a revelation.

A recent best-selling book, *Men Are From Mars, Women Are From Venus,* heralds the point that men and women are different. You're kidding! After decades in which certain groups have tried to tell us that men and women are the same, minus a few body parts, the truth finally resurfaces.

A while back, John Stossel of ABC's *20/20* newsmagazine reported on a TV special about all the differences between the two sexes. It was a relief to see someone in the secular media report on something so true—yet so often misreported.

And yet, I have to spoil these journalists' party. Because the true scoop was revealed much earlier than they realize. God Himself created and then declared the two sexes vastly different. "Male and female he created them" (Genesis 1:27).

In the creation account, the man was created from the dust of the ground; the woman was taken from his side. The man was given dominion over the animals; the woman was created as a completer of the man. He is incomplete without her.

As men, we love a lot of the differences. Although I enjoy my male friendships for camaraderie, shared interests, and the chance to do some guy talk, those friendships can't compare with that special relationship I have with Sheryl.

She is different from me, not just in the beautiful way God designed her body, but in the refreshing way she thinks, takes care of the children, talks with me, and cares for me.

Let's look at one simple example. Next time you go to a park, observe a mom and dad as they watch their son playing on a jungle gym. The father is encouraging his child to challenge himself by climbing to the top. The mother, on the other hand, may be telling her son to be careful. Together they achieve a balance.

HALFTIME POINTERS

How to Wow

➢ **Knock your wife over.** Instead of saying, "Let's go out tonight, honey," really ask her for a date. Arrange to change clothes after work somewhere else. Show up with flowers. Instead of asking, "Where do you want to go?" Say, "I have reservations for a great evening!" In other words, practice the art of romance.

➢ **Talk all day.** Dedicate an entire day to communicating with your wife. Don't pick up the paper. Don't watch TV. Just tell her you want to talk with her. Keep the lines open all evening without interruption. Take a walk. Go for a drive. You'll create a wonderful memory you'll talk about for years.

➢ **Consult short experts.** Ask your kids—seriously—how they think you're treating their mom? Is she happy? Do they see room for improvement? Be ready for some surprises. Ask them what you could do that she'd really love. Then let them help you pull it off.

This great advantage of two different people interacting so closely can create tension, though. Let's look at one common problem area: communication.

Communication is a key factor in marriage much as it is in football. One team that communicates well on the field is the San Francisco 49ers. Sometimes there almost seems to be telepathy in operation between Steve Young and receivers like tight end Brent Jones.

Jones also works on good communication at home with his wife, Dana. "Our communication has really improved," says Brent. "If there's a disagreement or argument-type of situation, we've learned not to control each other.

"I've learned to let Dana know what I'm thinking. If I can let her know more in depth what I'm thinking and why, and how I got to that point, it seems to diffuse any misunderstandings."

Sometimes when Sheryl and I don't see eye-to-eye, I get frustrated with her and want to say, "Why didn't you just come to me, lay it out, and we could have solved this problem?"

The obvious answer is this: Because my wife is a woman. She communicates in a way that is sometimes foreign to me. It takes too long, requires too many words, and is a bit too emotional for my taste. We men tend to grunt or use one-word syllables a' la Tim Allen, the tool man on *Home Improvement.*

"When you talk in the locker room, you can get away with anything, but when you come home, you have to learn how to talk 'woman.'"

BRENT JONES
SAN FRANCISCO 49ERS

If we're dedicated to honoring our children's mother and celebrating the differences between us, we'll learn to understand who she is and how to best honor her. We'll try to communicate with her respectfully, keeping in mind that it's our styles, not our goals, that are at odds sometimes.

For example, I used to get frustrated with Sheryl because our methods of saying good-bye were so different. If we were at someone's house for a visit and I felt that we might be wearing out our welcome, my protective personality makes me push to leave.

When I think it's time, I'll stand up, wave at our friends, and say, "Good-bye everybody." And I'm out the door.

A few minutes later, I'll still be in the car waiting for my wife to come out of the house. In my estimation, we're already late getting home so our school-age baby-sitter can get enough sleep for the next morning.

My wife's personality causes her to be concerned with the people at the home we're visiting. She has to go back and revisit every person and say good-bye individually.

I used to frown and honk the horn. But not anymore. I decided to be more tolerant of my wife's feelings, and if she wants to take a long time to say good-bye, why should I make her uncomfortable? I think about the positives in her personality, and I rejoice in her hospitality.

Imagine the example I'd set for my children if I would say to them, "You know, your mother is so gracious. Last night she took the time to talk with everyone at the party and say goodnight to them. I was so proud of her."

As men, we especially need to develop good listening skills. Generally speaking, women will use twice as many words during the day as men use. How can you find ways to bring your level closer to your wife's, while also working hard to be a good listener?

If we really want to honor our wives in front of our kids, and not get dropped for a loss in our marriage, we'll look for ways to capitalize on our differences. It's one more way we tell our children, "That mom of yours! She's one special woman!"

THE FOURTH DOWN: LAUNCH A SNEAK ATTACK ON THE LOVE ZONE

I want my children to know how important their mom is. And there are lots of ways I can show them.

I tell my kids all the time, "Do you know what? I love your mother so much! She's my best friend."

Often, I'll ask my children, "What can I do today to make Mommy happy?"

Or when it's Mother's Day, I'll ask, "What would Mommy really like for Mother's Day?"

Sometimes when I'm with my children and we're in the car, we'll stop by and pick up their mother some grocery store flowers. It doesn't cost a lot of money, but when I come home with flowers, their eyes beam with excitement to see their mother's reaction.

Retired Miami Dolphins offensive lineman and Super Bowl winner Norm Evans gave me a great idea. He said that whenever he was in a card shop, he'd buy a collection of greeting cards. Then, whenever he had to take an out-of-town trip, he'd use them to write notes to his wife Bobbe for no particular reason other than he loved her.

Earlier I referred to Kevin Glover of the Browns. Although at the time of this story, the Glovers didn't have any children, I'm sure in the years ahead it will demonstrate to their baby the depth of their love.

One thing you have to know is that during the 1994 football season,

Cestaine Glover was in the final stages of getting her law degree at a school in Maryland, and she was pregnant with their first child. Kevin was living in Detroit.

"It was during the holidays," he says. "We played at Miami on Christmas Day that year, so my wife knew I wouldn't be coming home. She was kind of down at the time, and she was staying at my parents' house—not expecting to see me anytime soon.

"The team came back from Miami and arrived at the Silverdome at 5:30 A.M. on December 26. I got a 7:00 A.M. flight out of Detroit to Baltimore and had a friend take me to my parent's house. Cestaine was upstairs when I got there. When she came into the bedroom, there I was, lying on the bed.

"I think she was pretty surprised! She had no idea I was coming home."

We can't all take long-distance flights to surprise our wives, but we can find exciting, creative ways to show our love.

Part of my children's security comes from knowing that I love their mother. It's practical, it's good, and it's biblical. Because we husbands are to love our wives as Christ loved the church, we are to love her as much as we love our own bodies. "He who loves his wife loves himself" (Ephesians 5:28).

THE TOUCHDOWN: RESPECT WILL SCORE EVERY TIME

My actions toward my wife should speak so clearly that my terms of endearment are bonus words. If I were to say, "I love your mommy," but treat her with disrespect, my words would be worthless. That would only teach my kids hypocrisy. If I want my example to count, I must treat my wife with loving care.

We also need to hold our children accountable for what they say and do to their mother. Good men stand up and protect their wives. But there's another reason. Your children will grow up to respect their own spouses.

I used to have a bad habit I still fight against. Sometimes friends or relatives would tease Sheryl in a dishonoring way, and I would join in the fun—or what I thought was fun. Little did I realize just how hurtful those words where.

I thought they were harmless firecrackers, but the truth is, I was tossing hand grenades and pelting my wife with shrapnel. Her spirit was wilting at my pleasure. Everyone but my precious wife thought it was funny.

I've learned how wrong this is, and I work to avoid repeat performances. I shudder to think what impact this kind of insult would have if my children heard it.

Let's look briefly at several other specific ways you can treat your children's mom with respect and honor:

• *Respect the power of anger—before you lose respect.*

You've heard, "Don't let the sun go down on your anger." But it's not always that easy to do. Try to work through conflicts as soon as the heavy smoke has cleared. Then both sides can begin discussion.

Anger puts a distance between husband and wife, and it lowers our feelings of love toward each other. Plus it can open the door for greater temptation outside of marriage.

Deal with conflict in front of the kids only enough so they know you can disagree—and still recover. But they shouldn't feel the trauma of watching two angry parents arguing.

• *Respect your wife's need to be touched—and to touch!*

You need to hug and hold and kiss your wife in the presence of your kids. A dad who does that will not only win his wife's heart but also his children's admiration. It's the kind of pure affection that children need to see.

And it's the kind of touching that our wives long for and appreciate. A pat here, a stroke on the face or forehead, a hug at the sink from behind. You can't give that gentle kind of love too much—or get it too much, either.

• *Respect your wife's need for leisure and family time.*

We try to go camping at least once a year. One time we had to set up a tent in the dark with a five-month-old baby. It was a tent that required two people, and there were three of us—one holding the baby.

Those are great memories—maybe hard at the time, but I revisit them fondly now. Those kinds of adversities you overcome together, and hopefully laugh about, and it makes your relationship stronger. Let your wife know this is important to you. Get away and have some fun—and some disasters, too.

• *Respect your wonder-wife by showing appreciation*

As I write this section, I'm in charge of our three kids. My wife is gone on a women's retreat.

While my wife calls this weekend a "women's retreat," I call it a Wife Appreciation Weekend. It isn't until we have to live in the world of another person that we really appreciate his or her perspective. I know lots of men who farm their children out when their wives go out of town.

On the one hand, especially today, I understand.

On the other hand, I'd recommend that once a year you have a Wife Appreciation Weekend. It will give her a break. And it will give you a greater appreciation and respect for your wife.

Our next subject is painful to discuss — especially after a discussion about honoring our great wives. But it's too big of a potential problem to ignore. I guess you could call it the ultimate act of *un*appreciation.

HOW TO NOT FORFEIT YOUR MARRIAGE

STAY FAITHFUL

In my line of work, I often see something going on that hurts me deeply. Athletes have become notorious for their womanizing and pursuit of sexual conquests. Among basketball players, we've got the outlandish claims of Wilt Chamberlain. And we were saddened to learn of the exploits of Earvin Johnson.

Let's be honest. Our society is pushing this kind of thing as hard as it can. Movies and television programming on prime time rarely celebrate a one-man, one-woman relationship. Commercials daringly portray scantily clad women.

These are the kinds of examples our children will see as they grow, no matter how hard we try to prevent it. They'll see so many idols having unashamed and seemingly harmless fun with sex that they'll be tempted to follow suit.

That's why as their primary role model, we need to guard our relationship with our spouse. We need to be one-woman kind of men.

A one-woman kind of man is committed with his eyes. A one-woman kind of man is committed with his mind. A one-woman kind of man is faithful with his lips. And a one-woman kind of man is committed with his feet.

Like Joseph in Potiphar's house, we will be on our toes, ready to "Flee from sexual immorality" (1 Corinthians 6:18).

None of us is exempt from this problem. That's why we need to keep our eyes focused on our wives. I for one don't want to have my head on a sexual swivel, gawking at the hottest fashions, bodies, and faces that walk across my path. Not only do I not want that, God doesn't either.

Guess who else is watching us watch — or not watch? Our sons and daughters need to know that we honor their mom by keeping our eyes focused on her. If we don't, we cannot be surprised when our sons follow our footsteps and view women as sexual objects.

I talked to Kevin Glover about his unusual situation of living in Detroit during the season while his wife lived in Baltimore. I was curious how he handled being a strong, well-to-do football player on his own in the big city—an easy mark for women who are on the prowl.

I asked Kevin, "How do you do that? I mean you get lonely, your wife is in Maryland, out of sight, out of mind."

"Oh, never out of mind. We always talk on the phone. We talk every day, sometimes two or three times a day."

"But you're a football player," I said, "and there's always women seeking. . ."

Kevin stopped me short. "You know better than that!" he said, a bit indignantly.

You know what? We all know better than that! Kevin's response was welcome. He wasn't interested in skirting the issue. He wanted me to know that he was, in truth, a one-woman man. Then he went on to talk about how he avoids those dangers I was alluding to.

"We both have a strong spiritual background," Kevin said. "We're both Christians, and we know what's right and what's wrong. When I'm in

Detroit, I go to work nine to five, eat dinner, see a movie, and talk to my wife.

"Also, we had a group this year on the team, a thirty-and-over group. There were just the four of us—Mike Johnson, Aubrey Matthews, and Leonard Burton, who isn't married. We'd get together after work, go out to eat, and head home from there.

"Part of it was accountability and not falling for the peer pressure. We were all in a similar situation. We sat around and had conversation. It's not like we went to dinner and moped and complained about not being able to see our spouses.

"We talked about how we grew up and how we met our wives or the season this year. Sometimes the conversation got deep. Usually it was just us four; at times we would invite other people along."

The group was helpful to Glover, yet the most important help was the faith he and his wife shared.

"We had a real trust, no doubt about it. We have the same faith. And she knew I wasn't going to be up here doing wrong. It's a security that you just don't have if you aren't a Christian. If you live apart like that, long distance, with the temptation of this business—without a strong foundation I think you're lost."

SACRIFICE TO WIN

Defensive players hate to sacrifice yards to the other team. But sacrificing some things—for your wife—is a good game policy.

Glover could have easily complained that his wife should have been with him and not back home going to school. Yet his wife had a dream. She wanted to become a lawyer, and Kevin honored her by sacrificing his desire for companionship for a few months.

A few years ago, I would not have understood how a guy could have done that. And furthermore, I would have probably told him he was wrong.

I remember going to Bible studies for years, and I would always thoroughly enjoy Ephesians 5:22, which says, "Wives submit to your husbands." I loved to read about submission—until I realized that the issue of submission wasn't an issue just for wives.

That's when I learned about Ephesians 5:21: "Submit to one another out of reverence for Christ." Now, I'd always been willing to give myself up for my wife. I would dive in front of a bullet if I thought I could take it and save her life.

But I discovered that to give myself up for her means more than just being willing to die for her. It means sacrificing what I want, for her sake.

My kids need to see me treat my wife that way. They need to see me give up my time, my interests, and my selfish goals in order to take care of their mom's needs.

To be honest, that hasn't always happened. I've failed Sheryl more than once, but I'll tell you about a particularly painful time early in our marriage.

Sheryl was pregnant for the first time and having medical problems. I went to the doctor's office with her and was waiting to hear the news. But there was a small problem, or what should have been a small problem: I had a raquetball appointment.

Sorry, honey. Gotta go. I left. She remembers (very vividly, I'm afraid) standing in the doctor's office and being told that she could not, would not have this baby. She would miscarry. It was just a matter of time. She drove herself home alone.

I wish this sad story ended here—and my selfishness, too. But it didn't.

I'd been a first round draft pick the year before but had held out. So this was my second year in the league but my first year to play. Sheryl began to miscarry the same day I was due at training camp. She begged me not to go. But I did, leaving her to have her miscarriage at my mother's home.

This is the schmuckiest thing I've ever done to Sheryl. Looking back now, I can't believe it happened this way. Why did I do it? I make no excuses, but I point to two reasons.

One, I was insensitive and dense so far as the emotional aspects of what Sheryl was going through. It wasn't happening in my body. And I just didn't realize how much Sheryl needed my support and comfort.

Second, I allowed myself to feel too much pressure from the football end of things. The situation seemed stacked up against me—and in the end, against Sheryl. The pressure to cave in was too much for me. I chose work over my wife.

Don't do it, guys. Your job is to sacrifice, to lay down your life, to love your wife—like your own body. This means feel what she's feeling, or at least try to. Don't put yourself in her place—*you'd* feel and react differently than a woman. Instead, really listen to *her* feelings about this place. And believe them.

Is this a sacrifice on your part? You bet. But her perspective should be worth that. Remember, you sacrifice to win.

Do you know the story of Anthony Muñoz?

Anthony, of course, was one of the greatest tackles of all time in the NFL. Early in their marriage, while Anthony was still at USC, DeeDee discovered that she had agoraphobia, the fear of the open marketplace. She constantly fears having panic attacks when she goes out of the home.

A lesser man than Anthony, knowing that he faced the NFL and all the fame and adulation that would follow, may have reacted in disgust. He may have decided that he didn't have time to worry about a wife with such a problem. Not Muñoz.

"I told Deedee, 'Whatever you go through, whatever I go through, we're both going through it together. We're going to fight this thing. Whether it's rehab on my knee, or you going through this agoraphobia—it'll be together.'"

For the Muñozes, sticking together has meant sacrifices on both sides. "If I had plans to go out and golf at one o'clock, and she couldn't handle me leaving, I would call my buddies and tell them, 'I can't golf today, something has come up.' I had no problem doing that.

"Sure there were sacrifices, but they weren't as big as the sacrifices she'd made during my last two years in school. She held a full-time job—a big sacrifice on her part.

"I know if it'd been just Anthony Muñoz—without God, I would have said, 'Hey, you're going to stay here, and I'm going to the golf course.' God gave me the compassion. I didn't really look on it as a sacrifice, and I really believe that comes from the Lord."

PRAY FOR YOUR BEST TEAMMATE

During a game against the New England Patriots one season, I gave up a couple of sacks. Our quarterback got deposited on the seat of his pants twice, and it was my fault.

On the plane ride home, one of my good friends on the team, Bryce Paup, sat next to me. He's a defensive pass rusher, so we work against each other on our game. He tries to improve his pass rush, and I try to improve my pass blocking.

As we cruised back toward Green Bay, Bryce asked me, "How did you play today?"

I said, "You know, I had a couple of bad plays, and I gave up two sacks."

Then I told him, "You know, for some reason it's the first time that I didn't lose my confidence."

It's really easy to lose your confidence when a guy beats you. You start wondering, *What am I doing wrong? What technique didn't I do right?*

Bryce looked at me in surprise and said, "You know, when you gave up that first sack, I was praying for you—specifically praying for your confidence."

From that point forward, Bryce and I began to pray for one another. When Bryce is on the field and the defense is out there, I pray for him—and vice-versa. It's amazing the intensity of prayer that goes on between believers on the football team.

As I contemplated this recently, I began to wonder why I don't pray for my wife while she's out on the field every day—being the role model for our kids.

Why haven't I before prayed for her like I have for my teammates? She is, after all, my first, last, life-long, and favorite teammate. So now I have committed to pray for her, for patience, energy, motivation, her commitment, her sacrifice, her peace.

As I look back over the suggestions I've made in this chapter, I realize it's a tall order. That's why I like what Mike Singletary, formerly of the Chicago Bears, said about the task ahead of us as husbands.

"It was in 1985, the first year of my marriage to Kim, that I discovered

I couldn't be the great husband, man of his word, and man of God that I wanted to be unless I chose to serve God wholeheartedly. I suddenly realized that I couldn't do it on my own."

Like Mike, I need someone praying for me and encouraging me. That's why I appreciate my wife so much. She has willingly come alongside me and asked, "How can I help you make our team better?"

I honor her input because she has a different perspective, and she is tuned into those needs of our children. She gently lets me know what I need to work on and how I need to interact with our kids or others. Nine times out of ten, she's right on the money.

She models for me the kind of help I can be for her and for our children. And she reminds me of the kind of helper Howard Hendricks says we need.

"You need a Barnabas," Hendricks wrote. "That is, you need a soul brother, somebody who loves you but is not impressed by you. Somebody who is not taken in by your charm and popularity and to whom you can be accountable.

"Do you have anybody in your life who's willing to keep you honest? By the way, don't miss your wife's role in this regard. I've never been able to impress my wife and kids. I tried but my family, like yours, is only impressed by the reality of Jesus Christ in my life."[3]

My Barnabas is Sheryl, and I need to make sure my children know how precious she is to me. She is worth work, worth sacrifice, worth prayer. And she's rooting me on in person. Now that kind of love-training I'll sign up for any day.

PERSONAL TIME-OUT

1. Have I ever written a tribute to my wife? What would I want to say or write to her? What could I share out of that tribute with my kids?

2. How do I see my wedding vows as a lifetime commitment? How do I treat it as a contract I can void at will? Would there be any value in getting

my children together and telling them adamantly what their mother and I believe about divorce? What would that be?

3. What are three differences between my wife and me that bother me? Have I talked these differences over with her? What steps can I take to see that these differences are turned into advantages?

4. If my children were to rate how I treat their mother on a one-to-ten scale with ten being "like a queen" and one being "like dirt," what would they say? Am I willing to ask them that question? Am I willing to ask my wife that question?

5. How am I a good role model for my kids in relation to how they should treat their future spouses? What are the three good characteristics my kids might see in me?

RUETTGERS' REFLECTIONS

Football truths that also work in real life

If you don't know your assignment, you can't carry out your assignment.

Obstacles are what you see when you take your eyes off your goals.

It's the total package that counts.

It's a long season. A lot will happen between now and the end.

PART FOUR

Game Analysis: Sizing Up Role-Model Success

CHAPTER TEN

How Do I Know I'm Winning?

My dad is the one that has influenced me the most. He always encourages me to be a man of goodness and knowledge.

—A TEENAGE BOY

One reason I like football is that you have instantaneous feedback. Throughout a game, for instance, you get continual reinforcement that you're doing well. If you create a hole in the defense and your running back blisters through for a big gainer, you don't have to wait for a writer to review your great blocking the next day in the paper.

And of course, when the game is over, you know immediately whether your effort resulted in a win or a loss.

With parenting the outcome is anybody's guess. Well, maybe that's a bit extreme. But the unknown future of our kids makes the job of being a father difficult. We can't be certain that the product of our efforts is bearing fruit.

Do you sometimes wish for just a glimpse into the future?

As we contemplate these mysteries, we can find some comfort in the Bible. For instance, we're told that God's Word, once we implant it in our children's lives, will not return to us without making an impact (Isaiah 55:11).

Proverbs 22:7 reassures us that if we train a child in the right way, he will return to it. Of course, this principle doesn't guarantee perfection in the child-raising process.But it does give us hope for the future and faith that our efforts matter.

We've covered a lot of ground in this book. We've seen how important our role is, what characteristics we should possess, how to grow spiritually, and what a game plan might look like. But what we really can't do is design a tool that guarantees our children will grow up the way we want.

None of us knows now how our children will respond to the gospel and the Holy Spirit's work in their lives. This is because God gave our children the same free will He gave us. And this is a gift to rejoice over.

A PARENT'S DARK DREAM, A BOY'S SEARCH FOR LIGHT

I'm sure Paul Frase's parents didn't know the mess he would get himself into during his lifetime, despite their efforts. Paul, who toils as a defensive end and defensive tackle for the Jets, was raised by parents who thought they knew what they were doing.

Paul is a preacher's kid, and he admits that he "grew up knowing about the Bible and knowing right from wrong." He even says he "accepted the Lord as my Savior when I was eight or nine years old."

But Paul's saga reminds us not to judge too soon whether we're winning at this role-model game. Here's his story in his own words:

> At a young age, I had a tug in my heart to give my life to Christ and acknowledge Him as the creator of the universe. And through the years, I never missed a Sunday school. I went every week of my life until I was eighteen years old.
>
> By then, I had my license and I was able to play hooky and jump in the car without my parents knowing. I'd go to the beach with the gang.
>
> In high school, I'd already kind of gotten away from the heart relationship with Jesus. I started partying on the weekends after the big football games, and that's when the distance between us became greater. I continued this way through high school, and started to drink a little bit more.
>
> All through this time, though, my paths were being directed

by the Lord—whether I was following Him or not. He was putting everything in place for me.

I never had the dream to be a football player. I definitely wanted to go to college, but I never knew I could pay for it that way.

Anyway, the Lord put me in the right place. And He gave me abilities and the discipline of my parents. Things went along great in college in football. We ended up fourth in the country my senior year at Syracuse, playing Auburn in the Sugar Bowl.

We had the world by the tail, and we knew it. We proceeded to get into partying hard with alcohol, dabbling in drugs.

I think my parents had an idea that I was probably partying, because by the time I left for college, I was hanging around with a couple of kids who were older than me, and we were always going out and driving around.

Even toward the end of college, I still didn't really know that I could play in the NFL. But a friend of mine, Ken Green, got me involved with the Senior Bowl. I had a good showing, and it afforded me the chance to be involved in the draft.

My first few years in the league I spent partying hard, living in New York City year-round, and just living it up with the boys and having a good old time.

Unfortunately, I was having too good a time. I was a sixth-round pick, so I wasn't making all the money in the world. Yet I thought nothing of going into the city with the boys, renting a limousine, and dropping a few hundred bucks a night.

At the end of my second year, January 1990, I became ill. I had lost thirty-five or so pounds over the course of four or five weeks. It was a thyroid problem. It was another five months before the Jets actually diagnosed me with a hyperactive thyroid. Actually, I had Graves' disease.

There were times I would get up in the morning and look in the mirror and literally think I was losing my mind. It's a disease that affects you emotionally. Your body just starts to eat away at itself.

In May of '90 the doctors told me not to worry about the illness, that things would get back to normal. I was starting to feel a little tap on my shoulder about my faith. Again, all this time I thought of myself as, and was, a good guy. I didn't abuse people, but I was leaving God out.

I started having some heartfelt convictions.I knew that everything I was doing, the partying and all that stuff, was producing nothing good. And I knew it was happening because Jesus Christ wasn't the center of my life.

I was drinking probably four or five nights a week during this time. That summer I remember going home to New Hampshire and attending church with my parents. I wanted to just sit and cry. I knew my spiritual life wasn't right, that I wasn't being a good influence on anybody.

I was out drinking with the boys one time, I think it was St. Patrick's day of 1991, and I blew up and said some things I never should have. A friend of mine, a non-Christian friend, witnessed the whole thing. He approached me a day or two later, and said, "Paul, you're changing. I never would've expected you to do that or say those things."

It hit me like a ton of bricks. The Lord was using that instance, that friend, to bring me back to my senses. I thought of all the rotten things I'd done, and all the people I'd offended. I just wished I could say I was sorry to every one of them for what I did. But I couldn't.

I knew alcohol had started to consume and control my life, and I didn't like what was happening. In early August, the big comeback year for me from the Graves' disease, everybody was wondering if I could really return. That's when I heard Steve Camp's song about living dangerously, and I fell on my knees and turned my life over to Jesus Christ.

Through praying to the Lord and trusting Him, He delivered me from the bondage of alcohol. Since that time, I've messed up a couple of times. But I know the truth and I know that the Lord has ultimate control. I've recommitted my life to Christ, and I'm giving Him a chance to fine-tune His work.

One thing that really impressed me about my dad throughout his life was that he just showed the love of Christ, and it was not condemning or judgmental. I think that was a big part of what eventually brought me back, the assurance of my parents' love.

When I talk to kids now, I stress to them the head knowledge is not what it's all about. It's having Christ in your heart. It took me eighteen years to realize that, from eight years old to twenty-six years old. It was a long time for me. It doesn't have to be that long.

I appreciate the legacy my Christian parents left through a sound upbringing. I'll never forget how every time I messed up and deserved a spanking, my dad would sit me down and tell me "This is going to hurt me more than it's going to hurt you," and he would explain what I did wrong.

Now that I'm old enough to understand and look back on it, I realize he was showing me the love of Christ with disciplinary, father-like understanding. But my father isn't perfect. I remember thinking, from a child's standpoint, "Oh, boy, I'd never be like that."

Through all my difficulties, my mom has been very sensitive. Other than I didn't have a big inheritance to spend, I see my life as a picture of the prodigal son. My parents had open arms when I came back to them.

If we think back about one of Paul Frase's insights during his time of being out on his own, we see one clear reason we dads must never give up on our children. Paul realized that while he was not walking the right pathway, God still had His hand of direction on Him.

That's something we dads need to keep in our thinking. We see the externals—what our children do, where they go, who their friends are, what they do. But we don't see nor can we actually know how God is working in our children's lives.

With some of the football players I've talked to, their parents always knew where they were spiritually. Guys like Herschel Walker and Reggie White. But we learn from Paul's story that in God's eyes, no one is a lost cause as long as he still has life and breath.

Think about it another way. When we read about heroes and role models, we often read about a particular incident in their lives that stands out as heroic or especially admirable.

"With football you have instantaneous feedback. With parenting, the outcome is anybody's guess"

KEN RUETTGERS
GREEN BAY PACKERS

For instance, we think of Thomas Edison as the man who almost single-handedly brought us into the modern age by inventing the incandescent light, the phonograph, the telegraph, and the first movies.

But we don't often think about the struggles that preceeded his moments of glory. We don't dwell on his hundreds of failed experiments.

Our children, like Edison, will have both successes and failures. They need to know that we will continue to guide them through godly role modeling no matter which way they seem to be going.

Are we winning? We don't always know. But we know this for sure, God has the power to make winners of even the most wayward child. And we have the ability to show the way if we keep at the job.

We can always have confidence that a loss today doesn't mean ultimate defeat. For instance, in football we can lose a few plays but still win the game. We can lose a game and still win the season. We can lose a season but still win in our career.

I think it's important to recognize that there are ups and downs in fathering and role modeling. The game is never over till it's over.

In the meantime, as we await the results of our role modeling, there will be times when our own love seems to run dry. As dads, we simply don't have unlimited resources. We give and give, trying to make sure we produce winners, and we can easily begin to run on empty.

When parents weep, there is a greater love.

When children lose their way, a greater love.
When wives cry out and men have lost their dreams,
There is a greater love.
There is a greater love,
There is a greater love,
When tears pour out, there is a greater love.
When healing does not come, a greater love.
When sorrows flow and joy is swept away, there is a greater love.
There is a greater love, there is a greater love.
God's love is greater than a father's because it comes from an infinite, all-loving being who knows the end from the beginning.

Are we winning? Are we losing? It's a tough call. Much tougher than any NFL referee ever had to make. He calls what he sees, using a definitive set of rules as his guide. We can't call our parenting a success or failure because we can't see beyond today.

Yet there are some benchmarks of success that we can look for, small bits of good news that might give us hopeful anticipation. See if some of these indicators help you know the game's still up for grabs.

BENCHMARKS OF SUCCESS

WHEN YOU SEE ONE POSITIVE STEP

Have you ever had a bad dad day? If you could turn in your dad badge, you'd be more than willing to. The kids argue with every statement you make. They aren't happy unless they're not happy with each other. They refuse to be content, no matter what you try.

That's the day you need to look closely for One Positive Step.

It's a little like in football when the other team has everything going its way. They're moving down the field as if it were a conveyor belt, and you couldn't stop them with a howitzer. Big ol' Momentum is on their side and all seems lost.

Then suddenly one of their guys gets carried away and facemasks you with the ref standing right next to you. Suddenly, the opponents just lost fifteen yards, and you see a bit of light beginning to break through. You've stumbled on One Positive Step.

The key for your team is to build on it. Put the extra effort in on the next play to make another good thing happen. Soon, that One Positive Step leads to a big play, and Momentum moves over to your side.

It just takes that first good step. At home—or whenever you have your modeling shoes on—force a turnover. Then look for the second step, then the third, and soon, at least the smell of victory will be in the air...

That is, unless it's a *really really* bad dad day.

In that case, just read on.

WHEN YOUR KIDS WANT TO BE LIKE YOU

The life verse of a role model should be 1 Corinthians 11:1. Paul, a pretty good example in his own right, said, "Follow my example, as I follow the example of Christ."

We all have those moments—whether our children want to drive the car like us (that can be scary) or comb their hair like we do. We're thrilled. And of course, the older the children in question, the more meaningful their imitation.

The Christian group Phillips, Craig, and Dean has a great song that reminds me how I want my kids to see me. The song is called "I Want To Be Just Like You."

He climbs in my lap for a good night hug,
He calls me Dad and I call him Bub.
With his faded old pillow and a bear named Pooh,
he snuggles up close and says, "I want to be like you."
I tuck him in bed and kiss him good night, tripping over the
toys as I turn out the light,
And I whisper a prayer that someday he'll see he's got a father
in God cause he's seen Jesus in me."

Chorus:
Lord, I want to be just like you

Cause he wants to be just like me,
I want to be a Holy example
For his innocent eyes to see.
Help me be a living Bible, Lord,
  that my little boy can read.
I want to be just like you, cause he wants to be just like me.

Got to admit I've got so far to go,
  make so many mistakes and I'm sure that you know. Sometimes
  it seems no matter how hard I try,
  with all the pressures in life, I just can't get it all right.
But I'm trying so hard to learn from the best,
  being patient and kind filled with your tenderness.
Cause I know that he'll learn from the things that he sees,
  and the Jesus he finds will be the Jesus in me.

Right from where he stands,
  I may seem mighty tall
But it's only because I'm learning
from the best father of them all.[1]

WHEN YOUR KIDS TALK ABOUT GOD

My family was taking a plane trip to Oregon. We were about to take off from the Milwaukee airport when I noticed my son attempting to talk to a fellow passenger. Matt and Sheryl were sitting in a row next to an elderly woman.

I watched and listened as Matt leaned forward, looked past his mother sitting next to him, and said to the woman passenger, "Excuse me, are you a Christian?"

It was a great blessing to hear that from my son. And it was a great challenge. I wish I had the courage to say things like that.

The lady answered Matthew, "Oh, yes I am."

So he asked her, "I'm going to pray. Would you like to pray with me that we don't die on this flight in a crash?"

When Matt took it upon himself to witness to a total stranger, I knew that God was really involved in his life. This is the kind of victory each of us dads want to see in our children. In that moment, we wonder if we're not winning, after all.

A friend once asked me how many children I wanted to have. I explained my fear of bringing more children into our troubled and disintegrating society.

My friend, who at the time had four children, answered me wisely when he said, "I agree with you, but the world needs good people in it, too. And I'm raising my children to be good, positive lights in this world."

He's right on. And we'll know we're making gains as parents when we see our kids talk about God—on their own.

WHEN YOUR KIDS ARE...WELL, GOOD

In America, we've become people who are wrapped up in the pursuit of happiness. I think if you ask a mother in our country today what she wants for her children, she'll say she wants their happiness.

If you asked an American mother forty years ago, she'd probably have said, "I want him to be good," meaning righteous. We have gone from a society raising righteous children to a society trying to raise happy children.

Happiness is a treasure, but it's also so elusive.

When we raise kids whose life's pursuit is happiness, they'll strive for things, activities, and relationships that will serve their own purposes alone. Righteous children, by contrast, will look for things, activities, and relationships that will help them serve God and others.

And they'll probably end up truly happy, too.

Plain old want-to-do-good children are one of the greatest blessings we'll ever see. And the quality of goodness in your kids is nothing less than a good sign.

WHEN YOUR WIFE GIVES YOU "THUMBS UP"

I can't emphasize enough how valuable my wife's input is to me as we raise our children. Sheryl is so much more than an interested observer. She knows me better than anyone else, and she knows my parenting

HALFTIME POINTERS

Hashmarks for Dads

➢ Protect yourself from perfect families. You know them: they dress right, say the right things, and go the right places—or so it seems. But measuring your family against them, especially on your bad days, can be deadly. How do you cope? Accept your own family's quirks, learn from families you admire, believe God is at work in you and the ones you love today, and He loves you—just the way you are.

➢ Choose your yardstick carefully. We all want some way to gauge how our children are "turning out." But one event or phase—a bad grade, a bad day, a foolish choice, a hard year of transition, being a teenager—doesn't signify parenting success or failure. Keep the long view firmly in mind.

➢ Refresh your parenting perspective each year. Take a class, read a book, attend a seminar to brush up on your father skills. A parenting group is also a good way to stay in touch with and be encouraged by other parents who face similar challenges. Three recommended books: *The Shaping of a Chrisitian Family,* by Elisabeth Elliot, *The Key to Your Child's Heart,* by Gary Smalley, and *Preparing for Adolescences,* by James Dobson.

weaknesses and strengths.

Therefore, hearing her feedback about my modeling is a great tool. Many times, when I'm not aware of failing or succeeding as a father, Sheryl steps in and helps me understand how I'm winning. And I try to return the favor for her.

This encouragement through teamwork is one way we can help each other make sure that we're still in the game.

We all prefer instant gratification to delayed gratification. But with children, our ultimate results are a long time coming. Of course, we get little glimpses of victory along the way. But the final accounting for our role modeling comes even later than the first.

If you're consistent in living a well-modeled, godly life for your family, you'll face the incredible prospect of standing in heaven someday before the King of kings and Lord of lords and hearing him say, "Well done, thou good and faithful servant."

As an athlete, I'm working hard to win football's ultimate prize, the Super Bowl. But even a Super Bowl ring would pale quickly in comparison to hearing my Lord tell me that I was faithful in modeling Him to Matthew, Katherine, Susan, Sheryl, my teammates, my friends, and anyone who even remotely came in contact with Ken Ruettgers.

Now, that's winning!

PERSONAL TIME-OUT

1. So far as fathering, do I feel like I'm winning, losing, or just keeping things even? Why? How do I measure my progress?

2. How would I handle the situation if I was in Paul Frase's parents' shoes? Would I have been as patient and long-suffering?

3. What positive steps have I seen my children take recently? How can I reinforce those steps?

4. How much of my concern for my kids is also tied up in concern about my appearance and reputation as a parent? How can I change that? Is my concept of "winning" correct?

RUETTGERS' REFLECTIONS

Football truths that also work in real life

The team that finishes strong at the end will win.

Leave it all on the field, except regrets.

It's very difficult to work on getting better in more than one area at a time.

When they quit coaching, then you know you're in trouble.

There is no "I" in team.

CHAPTER ELEVEN

When the Home Team Needs a Comeback

I admire my grandpa because of everything he has worked for and how he has overcome all the hardships put before him.

—SARA, A FOURTEEN-YEAR-OLD

Being behind—Yuck!

There's nothing worse than coming out of the tunnel for the second half of a football game when you're behind. As you run out onto the field, you're thinking about all the ground you need to re-take, all the hits you'll need to make and take—the plain, hard work. If you're still behind late in the fourth quarter, it get's worse—you're forced to run the grueling two-minute offense when you're most fatigued.

All this isn't to nail down a win; it's just to try to catch up, to get back in the game, to get *another chance* to win.

It's the same for dads, really. Some of you need to make a comeback on a large scale.Others of you need to make a comeback once a week. The good news: both can be done. They just take a little extra effort.

THE KING OF COMEBACKS

If we're going to talk about comebacks and football, we can do no better than to talk to the King of Comebacks. His name is Frank Reich, quarterback of the Carolina Panthers. Reich is the architect of the greatest comeback in college football history. And the greatest comeback in pro football history!

While playing for the University of Maryland, Reich brought the Terrapins back from the dead. In a game against the University of Miami, Maryland was behind at halftime, 31-0. That's when Coach Bobby Ross inserted Reich into the lineup. When the dust settled, Maryland had won 42-40.

Then, while with the Buffalo Bills, Frank orchestrated a spectacular come-from-behind victory over the Houston Oilers after being behind at the half by thirty-two points. In that game the halftime score was 35-3. Frank went to work, and led his team on a charge that ended in a 41-38 triumph.

I talked with Frank recently about his incredible comebacks to get some perspective on what it takes to win when all the odds seem to be against us. Here's what he told me:

"Prior to the Houston game—the Wednesday before that Sunday game—my sister called to tell me about a song called, 'In Christ Alone.' She said I would enjoy it, so I listened to it on Wednesday night before that game.

"I was really moved by the song, so much that between then and the Sunday game, I must have listened to it a hundred times. During the course of the game, each time after we would come off the sideline, I was on the sidelines humming 'In Christ Alone.'

"Obviously, I was thinking about what we needed to do on the field, but the song had been so ingrained that I couldn't get it off my mind.

"I'll never forget the words. The words I recite most often are, *'In every victory, let it be said of me, that my source of strength and my source of hope is Christ alone.'*

"I thought at the time that the song had meaning for me for that one day, that one game, and that was it. Later, I realized that the song has application in my life every single day. It's not about the greatest comeback in the NFL, but the everyday Christian life.

"Through Christ alone we have the strength and hope that we can overcome any circumstances, whether we're behind thirty points in a football game, whether we've just lost our job, whether something terrible has happened in our family, or whether we face problems in our marriage.

"I really believe that even when things seem at their worst, we can still overcome through the power of Jesus."

GOOD NEWS FOR UNDERDOGS

This is great news for us role models. Role models always need to come back. No matter how hard we try in this life to be the men God wants us to be, we always seem to end up stumbling, losing ground.

I admire role models who are willing to admit that they're sinners who cannot profess to be perfect. I think that's a strong quality and one that can be understood and admired by young followers.

We're all in the same boat. I don't always make the right decisions, but I'm striving toward modeling Christ as a husband and as a father. I don't come to you writing this book as a perfect example—it's not like some financial seminar where the guy up front has his finances all buttoned down.

As Paul says in Romans, "All have sinned and fall short of the glory of God." That's one of the great things I like about being a Christian—right off the bat, we can admit, "Hey, I'm not perfect. But I'm redeemed, and I sure am trying."

The truth is, our children can learn a lot when they see how failure affects us and how we overcome adversity. After a Packer game, I often find myself talking to my kids about winning and losing. When I come home and the team has lost badly, we talk about it.

The conversation might go something like this: I tell them that, yes, it's very disappointing to lose. Yes, I've put a lot of hard work and study and practice into winning, and I no, I didn't accomplish my goal. Yes, losing is hurting our chances of going to the Super Bowl, which is one of the goals I work very hard for.

We talk about the fact that it is very difficult to win, and it's almost impossible to win all the time. Winning matters—and that's why you always get up and try again.

Football's been a blessing to our famliy in this way because when I give up a sack or receive a penalty or come home after a loss, we have instant lesson time.

Sure, I want my kids to see me bounce back. And I want them to see me go on to win. But in the big scope of things, I'm learning that when life brings disappointments, important lessons come along, too.

In a football game, if you're four touchdowns behind but you end up losing the game by a touchdown, it's still a loss. But in life, coming from far behind and improving isn't always a loss. It's often a step in the right direction toward victory down the road.

In fact, the only real way to make true gains with your kids during a comeback is one step at a time. A huge overnight try-to-change-everything-immediately tactic probably wouldn't have much staying power.

And it probably wouldn't be trusted by your kids, either.

Are you ready to try again? You've got nothing to lose and your kids have much to gain.

HOW TO LAUNCH A COMEBACK

CONFESS YOUR FAILURES

Failures have a way of putting the big issues in a clear light—like what it takes to get back up, ask for forgiveness, and set about to make things right again.

Depending on the age of your kids, you may need to actually sit down with them and say something like, "I think I've blown it, kids. I love you so much, but I've made mistakes. And I want to start to improve by asking for you to forgive me...."

Don't be afraid to be specific about how you feel you've failed them. They won't respect you less, but more.

In 1927, Babe Ruth hit a record sixty home runs in a season, a record that would stand for thirty-four years; yet in the same season he set another record for strikeouts. Abraham Lincoln became our most revered president—only after a series of failures in business, politics, and private life. Benjamin Franklin, Winston Churchill, and Albert Einstein had all been fired from their jobs at one time or another.

These great men of history picked themselves back up after their failure and went on to victory. We admire them more for their resilience and their perseverance.

So will your kids admire you.

CHOOSE RELATIONSHIP OVER POWER

In the home, problems can come from having a dysfunctional parenting style. In their book *The Hidden Value of a Man*, authors Gary Smalley and John Trent described four parenting styles that can be found in most homes.

There's the autocratic, in which a person—typically the father—will say, "You'll do it my way or else!" Then there's the permissive father, who says, "You can do anything you want." Far too often, there's the neglectful father, whose motto seems to be, "I really don't care what you do." And finally, there's the relational father. He says, "I'm listening, I care about you, I want to understand, this time we'll do it this way because..."

Obviously, the first three styles are destined to fail. Perhaps we need to look at our technique of modeling in the home and see if we might need to make a comeback in the way we interact on a regular basis.

> *"In 1927, Babe Ruth hit a record sixty home runs in a season, a record that would stand for thirty-four years, yet in the same season he set another record for strikeouts."*
>
> KEN RUETTGERS
> GREEN BAY PACKERS

INVEST IN YOUR TREASURES

Ever notice "childless couples"—with kids? I have. They're the ones who have children but don't seem to realize it. Honestly, it's easy for any of us to get in this situation on a busy week. But Sheryl and I try to think of it this way: invest in what you treasure.

Psalm 127:3 says, "Sons are a heritage from the Lord, Children a reward from him." We try to evaluate the value we place on the children God has entrusted to us. When things get out of whack—often for all the "right" reasons—we try to make the hard choices to get our time priorities in order.

Your kids are your treasure. Let them know that as you try to make improvements.

CHOOSE CONSISTENCY AND TRANSPARENCY

We can't hide our failures. Children especially see them. They may not always say anything now. But our actions are surely affecting them. This is borne out in an article directed at teachers and how students perceive them.

"According to students, teachers 'have to follow the rules themselves' in order to effectively teach character education.

"They have to be fair and real—not phony. 'Teaching moral values doesn't work,' students say, 'if teachers try to make a big deal or have a separate class about it.' It seems to me that values are caught not taught.

"Students from classrooms with 'poor models' report evidence of double standards and differential treatment. For example these teachers say things like 'you should be kind and respect others.' Yet, students report that they 'choose favorites.' 'treat us like babies,' 'don't listen,' and 'give us busy work.'

"Although these poor role models believe they are teaching respect, they're blind to the way their behaviors effect student learning and behavior. As several students put it 'teachers can't fake it.'"

REDEEM YOUR LOSSES

Sterling Sharpe, one of the best receivers in the National Football League, willingly admits to a mistake that will affect the rest of his life. It is the error so many young people are making today—and far too few are seeing as sin.

"I think one of the biggest mistakes I made was the fact that I know the Bible and I still I had a daughter before her mother and I were married. Sins are not measured by weight, but that's a sin.

"Now how can I go into somebody's high school and tell them about teen pregnancy? How can I tell them, 'Don't have these kids until you get married, or don't have premarital sex?' How can I do that? I can't. Because I made a mistake.

"But based on my mistake, I've asked for forgiveness and I've gotten it. I have a wonderful daughter. I made this mistake, but let's look at the big picture. I don't think Summer will ever go hungry or will wonder where her father is or ask why her dad does not influence her life.

"She is beginning to learn so much about not only herself, but about us as her parents. Which is really fun, and she's beginning to see and experience more. It's important to me to be able to get into her life when she falls, and not just to pick her up, but to say, 'Look, just because you fell, you're okay. Get up! No, I'm not going to help you up. You can stand up.'"

LOOK FOR GOD'S GOODNESS

Sharpe came back from an indiscretion called premarital sex and has come back as a person should. He admitted his mistake, asked forgiveness, and is now dedicating his life to taking care of his daughter and wife.

But he faces another comeback. He suffered a neck injury during the 1994 season that could have ended his football career. Now he deals with the struggles of recovering from that. His career is in the fourth quarter and he's in the two-minute drill. But he knows about coming back.

"The injury to my neck is a setback," says Sharpe. "With this injury, I might not get a chance to play anymore. But I know that regardless of what we pray for, God's will is going to be done in my life."

And Sterling told me, with all he's been through, he's learned that God's will is the big win he wants most for his life.

Comebacks are made of this.

RESPECT YOUR OWN SCARS

I don't know if singer Wayne Watson has faced any comeback situations in his life, but one of his songs clearly points to the best answer I can think of for how to come back. In Watson's "Friend of a Wounded Heart" he wrote:

> Jesus meets you where you are;
> Jesus, He heals your secret scars,

All the love you're longing for is Jesus,
the friend of a wounded heart.

Have you ever seen a pro football helmet at the end of a season? It is covered with battle scars. I've had some battle scars that are so deep I can look into them and recall exactly how I got them. A good battle scar will cut four to six inches long, and the gouge will show the color of the opposing team's helmet, ground right into the plastic.

Offensive lineman pick up most of their battle scars from protecting the quarterback, or from forging a trail for the running back. Defensive lineman and linebackers get their scars from tackling huge obstacles (the opposing offensive line) head on.

Every scar reminds me of something: a respected opponent, a big win, an unfortunate loss, a lesson learned.

In your personal life you may have some battle scars, scars that leave gouges so deep that you can peer into them and remember when, where, and how they happened. A scar is never a thing of beauty, but sometimes beautiful truths can be learned from them. Sometimes scars change us for the better—if we let them.

If an athlete gets gouged for a touchdown, should he quit? No way. Yet some of us men have pulled ourselves out of the game because of battle scars.

GET BACK IN THE GAME AS SOON AS POSSIBLE

God wants us back in the game. It's His game plan. He put you in charge of making the family calls and executing the plays. He made you the leader in the home huddle and on the field. And he gave you the homefield advantage.

And just like teammates relying on their quarterback, your family is counting on you to lead the way.

There are times in football when an injury requires medical attention, healing, and rehabilitation. But every player on the team knows how important the injured player is and wants him back on the field as soon as possible.

Perhaps you've been injured so badly by a battle scar that you need some time to heal. Do you need professional help to find healing? Then get it. Sometimes you can't come back without expert help.

Maybe you need to see a pastor or a Christian counselor, just as a football player sometimes needs to see the team physician. But don't let a setback, a scar, keep you out of the game.

PUNT AWAY THE PAST

If you've been neglecting your role as a hero in someone's life because of a failure, take heart in the story of Derrick Moore. His dad had neglected him as a kid, which, of course, did its damage.

Yet Moore made a comeback because he's done the hard work of letting go of the past.

"In my youthful days, I really didn't have male role models, men in my life that could influence me positively. My father wasn't in the home, so my mother basically raised all of us. No kid deserves that kind of neglect from a dad.

"But I have a pretty good relationship with my father right now. I can't go back to yesterday, nor can he, and we don't waste our time living twenty years ago. We try to spend as much time as we can in the present, and we do the things we can do now.

"The past is the past, and whatever happened in the past, that's exactly what it is. It's gone, and I want to walk in faith and trust that God will keep us until He comes."

> *"I can't erase the first-half score, but I can do everything in my power to make the second half better."*
>
> DERRICK MOORE
> DETROIT LIONS

Derrick inpsires me to make the most of the rest of my life. I can't erase the first-half score, but I can do everything in my power to make the second half better.

HARNESS REAL POWER

Whereas Frank Reich knows about single-game comebacks, Doug Dawson knows about career comebacks. After suffering debilitating injuries and sitting out several seasons, Doug Dawson refused to give up. With the help of his brother, he worked out diligently enough to win a place on the Cleveland Browns.

It's not hard to find one of Doug's secrets. Notice the incredible strength he found in making the Bible a power tool in his life.

"When I got hurt, one of the things that helped me stay positive the whole time was James 1:2–3—'Consider it pure joy, my brothers, whenever you face trials of many kinds, because you know that the testing of your faith develops perseverance.' That was something I memorized and thought a lot about.

"When I was trying to make a comeback, I used Philippians 4:13—'I can do everything through him who gives me strength.' I decided that I was going to work out as hard as I could. If God wanted me to have the opportunity to play again, I was going to play.

"I asked everybody—my girlfriend (who is now my wife), my brother, my family, and friends—to pray for the opportunity for me to play football again.

"During the comeback, I think probably my two favorite verses were Philippians 4:6-7, 'Do not be anxious about anything, but in everything, by prayer and petition, with thanksgiving, present your requests to God.' This is something I try to quote before I go out on the field even to this day.

"The only way I was able to get back up after that long of a layoff, and to keep my confidence and my spirits up, is because of my Christian faith. I felt a real peace. I had a positive, upbeat attitude because, as Romans 8:28 says, 'And we know that in all things God works for the good of those who love him.'"

For Dawson, then, his comeback rested squarely on God's shoulders. He clung to God's Word, he trusted God's power, and he was depending on God's will. That's a comeback formula that works—even if we are not coming back to the NFL.

IT'S GOD'S KINDNESS THAT LEADS US

I know about a role model who was so popular that the women of his land were singing about him, bragging about the fact that he was a better warrior

HALFTIME POINTERS

Smart Ways to Start Again

➢ Here are some things that won't work when you need a family comeback:

• placing blame; • holding grudges; • flogging yourself; • keeping scores of grievances; • giving up; • ignoring problems.

➢ Adjust your expectations. When you're trying to make a comeback, you want to see change fast—not just in yourself, but in those you're working hard to impress. This can be disappointing. Focus on your own efforts, not your family's response.

➢ Reestablish trust. Look for ways to show your family that you can be counted on and that you mean what you say. Only make promises you know you can deliver on. Be specific: "Tomorrow at 4:00 P.M., I'll take you to the park." Then follow through.

➢ Focus on one challenge at a time. In your enthusiasm to make a comeback, it'd be easy to attempt too much. Change takes time, like muscle-building. Choose one area that you feel is "flabby," but are ready to excercise. Controlling your anger? Helping your wife around the house? Focus on only that for now.

than the king. For years, this man was the most recognizable guy in the country. No doubt he was the trendsetter of the decade.

His name was King David. A man after God's own heart, he was called. A great role model King David. Yet even David didn't escape being less than perfect. He had his problems, too. He committed adultery, had his lover's husband killed, and then married her. Pretty nasty stuff, I'd say.

And this was "a man after God's own heart." His kids must have felt pretty lost, with no one to look up to. Did David, who had fallen so far, quit? Not on your life. Check out his comeback prayer in Psalm 51:

> Create in me a pure heart, O God,
> and renew a steadfast spirit within me.
> Do not cast me from your presence
> or take your Holy Spirit from me.

Restore to me the joy of your salvation
and grant me a willing spirit, to sustain me.

The Bible says God will never despise the prayer of repentant man. No matter how far down we are, God will hear our prayers for help and release His power on our behalf to get us back on track.

Listen to Eugene Robinson of the Seattle Seahawks as he talks about the only way to make a comeback that will last.

"I tell you what. God's forgiveness through Jesus was the key to why I became a Christian. I was forgiven for the junk and all the stuff that I've done. I didn't understand the magnitude of that forgiveness. He forgave me for everything I ever committed. I thought it was a bargain that was too good. Christ paid for every sin that you could ever commit, from past to present to future.

"For a guy who thinks he's beyond a comeback, that he will never be able to rise from the bottom of the barrel, I'd tell him that's a lie. If you're stuck in sin, God is patient."

EUGENE ROBINSON
SEATTLE SEAHAWKS

"For a guy who thinks he's beyond a comeback, that he will never be able to rise from the bottom of the barrel, I'd tell him that's a lie. If you're stuck in sin, God is patient. He's wanting you to say, 'Here I am, Lord.' He's not there to beat you down. He will discipline you, yes, but He doesn't want you to perish.

"God is saying, 'Gene, turn around, and come home.' So for anybody—I don't care what you've done, I don't care how bad you are, I don't care if you've killed people, stole—Christ paid for your sins. And what you need to do is call out to God for His forgiveness."

It really is that simple, guys. Don't be a do-it-all-alone ball hog type of father. Share the load with your Lord. It's God's kindness that leads you to repentance. And His mercy will lead you to a comeback.

PERSONAL TIME-OUT

1. In what areas have I fallen behind right now in my role modeling? Who is suffering because I'm not doing the job?

2. What is an example of something in my past that could have threatened my example to my children if I hadn't given it over to God, asked His forgiveness, and moved on?

3. When I look at the battle scars I've accumulated as a dad and as Christian in general, what do I learn from them? Do they make me want to quit or to keep going? How can I make sure I keep going?

4. Have I given myself completely to Jesus Christ, the only source of forgiveness for my wrong actions? If I asked for His forgiveness as Savior, have I also given my life to Him as Lord?

RUETTGERS' REFLECTIONS

Football truths that also work in life

If you lose your composure in the battle, you'll lose the war.

How you react to failure determines the true champion in you.

Every one gets beat, even the best of the best.

It's not over till it's over.

If you can't see yourself win, then you probably won't.

PART FIVE

MVP Awards: Honoring Role-Model Heroes

CHAPTER TWELVE

Fathers Hall of Fame

My mom is my greatest role model because she pulled me out of my darkest time. She helped me realize I don't have to be another face in the crowd.

—THIRTEEN-YEAR-OLD GIRL

It was a Sunday evening, and we were preparing to host the Denver Broncos in a TNT Sunday evening telecast. Of course, we always get a little more pumped for a game in which we are the only two teams on national TV—Sunday, Monday, and Thursday night contests.

But it wouldn't matter to my friend Tunch if we were playing at 3:00 A.M. on Tuesday in front of no one. He is always ready.

"This is the biggest game of my life!" Ilkin shouted as we dressed for the Denver game, and his voice bounced off the locker room walls.

We had just acquired Tunch, but we'd already come to look forward to his pregame ritual. Like clockwork, he always gave this same message before every pregame warmup.

It was an important reminder to us that every game is indeed the most important game of our lives. And by extension, every play is the most important play of our lives.

This particular game with the Broncos was important to us because we had dug ourselves into a hole in the standings. It was a possible turning point in our season. If we lost, we might never recover; if we won, we could be back on the playoff road. How right Tunch was!

Taking his cue, we came out in championship form. At halftime, we had things firmly in hand, leading 30-7. Yet even as we enjoyed that lead, we knew that the Denver Broncos had a guy at quarterback who specializes in coming from behind.

We knew that John Elway wasn't a quitter.

Sure enough, Elway brought his team back. With only a couple minutes to go in the game, we were up by just three points as the Broncos got the ball at midfield. Our faithful fans knew as well as we did that the situation looked scary, so they began to shout encouragement to the one man on the field who they felt could save the Pack.

"Reggie!" the shout began. Then louder. "Reggie! REGGIE!!"

The Packer faithful were pleading with Reggie White to sack Elway and keep Denver out of field goal range.

It'd been a long night for White. He had to be tired.

But perhaps he was encouraged by the memory of Tunch yelling, "It's the biggest game of my life." Perhaps he was driven by his determination to give his best for God. Surely he heard the fans pleading for him to do something heroic.

For whatever reason, Reggie responded as he usually does. When it counted most, he came up with first one sack of Elway and then another. The Bronco drive was stopped, and we had the victory.

In this particular "biggest game," we had prevailed.

As we walked off the field in triumph, we were victorious gladiators—tired but happy men congratulating each other and reveling in the victory.

Suddenly amid the noise, I heard a familiar little voice call out, "Dad!" I looked to the sideline and there was my son, Matthew, dressed in a minature version of my number 75 jersey, running toward me. I picked him up and gave him a huge Green Bay Packer hug.

I happened to glance up and notice that Matt and I were being shown on the big screen scoreboard above the stadium tunnel. Everyone in the stadium was reveling in this magic moment. I put Matthew down, and we walked hand-in-hand toward the locker room, beaming from ear to ear.

It's a great feeling to share victory with someone you love.

As I iced down my muscles that night and as Matthew made his usual locker room rounds, I reflected on this marvelous night. I thought about what Tunch had said and how every week seemed like the biggest game of our lives. And I remembed watching Matthew run to greet me on the field.

Sitting waist-deep in ice, I pictured my family. Matthew. His sisters. My wife.

It became clear to me that aside from my relationship with Jesus Christ, my family was the biggest game of my life, and every day with my family is the most important because I don't know which one will make the most difference to them.

During which day and during which moment with my kids would I say something to them that would lead them triumphantly through life?

Looking back on that season now, we know how important that Denver victory was. It opened the way for us to turn our season around and make the playoffs. In fact, we made it to the second round before losing to the eventual champion Dallas Cowboys. For the first time in twenty years of full-season action, the Pack had made the playoffs.*

Before the Denver game, no one could guess the impact of that game—and of Reggie White's performance—on the rest of the season.

Likewise as dads, we never know when the opportunity will arise to contribute to a turning point in a season of our children's lives.

As the chapters of this book have unfolded, I've tried to share a variety of things with you—facts, stories, Scripture, illustrations, and various other devices that I hope have given you encouragement.

In this final chapter, however, I'd like to take a different approach. I'd like to simply share with you some hero stories that I've accumulated. All these stories are about incredible dads who deserve to be celebrated.

None of them knew, day to day, how their efforts would pay off. But they heard God cheering them on, and they took advantage of their home field. They left behind a legacy that will impact generations to come.

*Green Bay made the playoffs in 1982, a strike-shortened season.

AVERY JOHNSON
SAN ANTONIO SPURS
LEGACY OF HIS DAD

"It's easy for me to honor him, because he was always there for me. We had a great father-son relationship. That's one reason I'm headed in the right direction as the father, husband, and man I need to be.

"Even in junior high and high school, my dad and I could talk about anything. I never feared he was going to punish me if I was honest with him.

"I never feared my dad was going to punish me if I was honest with him."

AVERY JOHNSON
SAN ANTONIO SPURS

"I've talked to teens who tell me they've had a good relationship with their fathers—but then they come up against something tough, and they think they should talk to their friends. I never had to do that.

"I can still hear Dad say, 'Shoot the ball.'

"In life, I can still hear him say, 'Choose the hard road. Don't go down that easy road you see the rest of the world go down. Be a leader. Never fear the criticism of men if you're doing the right thing. Do the manly thing. Serve God every day. That's how you reach your fullest potential.'

"What I can hear him say most of all is, 'Whatever you do, do it as unto the Lord, and God will reward you. You don't want this world giving you your reward, because the only reward that lasts is the one he will give.'"[1]

TERRY BOWDEN
AUBURN FOOTBALL COACH
LEGACY OF HIS DAD

Terry Bowden talks about the things his father, Bobby Bowden, national champion coach at Florida State, taught him.

"First, the beliefs and understanding of my faith in God came from Dad's work and example. He made it clear that everyone has his or her own choice to accept or reject. I know for certain my choice would have been more difficult to accept without him there. I understand what God asks of us as Christians because of him. Second, I've accepted the responsibility not to be afraid to let people know what I believe. My dad has always said, 'I'm in the spotlight now, and I want to honor God by not fearing what people may say if I open my mouth to talk about Jesus Christ.'

"The only thing bad about being Bobby Bowden's son is trying to recruit against him.

"He's the best coach in America, and without a doubt, the finest man I know."[2]

SEAN JONES
GREEN BAY PACKERS
GRANDPA'S LEGACY

"I grew up with my grandfather. I guess he was the most influential person in my life, because he taught me so much. He would always say, 'You should always pray for wisdom and knowledge and understanding.'

"He was a real spiritual person; he was a Christian. He used to make us all go to church. When you're a kid, sometimes you don't really want to go to church, but he stressed it. Everything he did in his life revolved around his faith, and anything he had he felt it was God-given.

"As a child, I didn't understand that, and we would make comments like, 'Next week, I'm going to do this,' and he always made the point, 'If God lets you.'

"He'd always say, 'Next year, if I live.' These little things he would say didn't make sense until I got older, then it started clicking.

"I think I listened to him, though, because when I came over here from Jamaica and saw the things he was able to accomplish with so little, I was impressed.

"We didn't have a refrigerator, so my grandfather would dig a hole and cement it, and that was our refrigerator. I thought he was the greatest thing. He wasn't very educated in terms of school, but he was so wise. He could spit out parables and phrases. I looked to him as being a very wise person.

"He was a real wise person in terms of interacting with people. He very rarely wrote, because he wasn't taught a lot. I guess he left school early when he was growing up, but he took a lot of time to read the Bible. He knew the Bible backward and forward. I really respected that about him.

"My grandfather died in my arms during my second year of college. That was real hard. I went through a daze for a couple of months, just sitting around moping. He died around Thanksgiving, so I basically blew off the rest of the semester.

"Finally, I decided I didn't want to let him down.

"He left a legacy. I still pray for wisdom, knowledge, and understanding, just like Grandpa told me to."

BILL BROOKS,
BUFFALO BILLS
DOING WHAT A DAD SHOULD DO

"My father never went to college, but he went to high school. He was a janitor in a hospital in Boston, and I was very proud of that. He got up at six in the morning and didn't get home until nine at night—every single day until I went to college.

"When I was younger, I didn't quite understand what it took to take care of our family, or why my dad was gone a lot. He'd come home late at night and say, 'Hi, Junior!' Then he'd eat, take a shower, and go to bed.

"Yet my dad was a big role model for me.

"As I got older, I realized his high school education only took him so far—yet he worked hard to provide for my mom and me.

"We were lower income, but we weren't dirt poor. Dad worked two jobs just to pay rent, get me some new clothes, and make his car payment. And that was it.

"As a kid, I didn't understand why he couldn't spend more time with me, but as I got older I realized he was doing what a man should do.

"Another thing that made me proud of my dad was the way he committed his time to me. He was always supportive of me. Even though the weekend was his time to catch up on sleep, he'd sacrifice that to go to my games. And as much as he loved cars, he'd give up time with his cars to be with me.

"Today, it seems many families have both parents working. Then they try to do hobbies and things after work. I don't think enough time is spent with the kids. Maybe they need family hobbies that they can all do together.

"We live in a hustle-bustle world. We try to get things done quick. Instead of sitting down together, we often eat our meals on the run, and consequently miss out on family talks around the table.

"As a kid, I missed a lot of that, too, but at least on weekends I got my dad's attention.

"When I went to college, my dad was still very supportive. I had a scholarship so he didn't have to worry about funding my education, and he was able to quit his second job. That made me feel really good. Dad had worked hard to save up for my tuition, and I didn't even need it. He could've taken that money and done whatever he liked. But you know what he did? He bought me a car.

"He wanted me to have a car. He gave it to me and said it was my responsibility to take care of it. I was thankful for the car but also for his faith in me to take care of it. I had to work during the summer to make money for the car, and it helped me grow up.

"He didn't throw me out in the world, and say, 'Go ahead and do it yourself.' Instead, he helped me."

WILLIAM WHITE
DETROIT LIONS
LEGACY OF A HARD-WORKING DAD

"Every day, my dad would go to work at 4:00 a.m. everyday. It was fifty-five miles one way. Whether it would rain, sleet, or snow, he went to work.

"When I was really young, I thought all parents did that. But as I got older, in junior high or high school, and I'd hear about other parents, I realized he was different. He was special. I really admired him for that.

"I was in college when my dad finally got his high school diploma. He did that because he thought it was right and what he needed to do to help raise us kids and show us the right way.

"When I visited my dad at work, I was in awe. And that's one of the things that made me choose metallurgical engineering as a field of study. I always liked engineering. When I went up to General Motors and watched that iron being poured, I saw that it was all dirty and hot in there. When I realized that my dad had been coming up there for thirty-six years, I was even more impressed.

"The unions were strong, and my dad didn't have to go to work every day. They got sick days, they could call in or whatever, and they're protected by the union. But he told me he went in to work because that's what Jesus would do. He wasn't just being a role model for us, but he was trying to live the godly life he preached to us."

BRIAN KINCHEN

CLEVELAND BROWNS

DAD AND THE CANDY TRUCK

"My dad used to deliver Tom's Candy in an old truck with sliding doors and tall seats. One day he took me with him to make his run.

"I remember how the passenger side of the van had no seat—just a pole where the seat should've been. My dad turned over an empty candy box and put it on the pole. Then I sat on the box.

"We rode with the doors open, and of course, there was no seat belt. My dad took an extra fast turn, and I went straight out the door. I didn't remember another thing until I woke up in the hospital.

"To this day, my father jokes that I have a subconscious thing against him because of that incident. But I just remember the huge thrill I got whenever I rode with my dad in his truck, doing his job. And how every time he brought the truck home, we'd get bubble-gum cigars, peanut-butter logs, and other great treats.

"As a kid, I had my heroes that I looked up to, but they were more like images. I knew they were actual people, of course, but I just watched them on TV. They weren't real. On the other hand, my father was reality. He was there everyday."

RUSSELL MARYLAND
DALLAS COWBOYS
LEGACY OF PARENTAL PROTECTION

"If it was up to my peers, I wouldn't have amounted to much as a football player. You know how cruel kids can be with the fat jokes and everything.

"But my parents definitely helped me. My parents always told me that family came first. The only people I needed to seek approval from was my mother, my father, and God.

"If it was up to my peers, I wouldn't have amounted to much as a football player."

RUSSELL MARYLAND
DALLAS COWBOYS

"As I grew older, I grew more cognizant that this was true. Even though somebody called me fat, or if someone didn't expect a whole lot out of me because of my weight, I knew regardless of what I did, as long as I lived life righteously, I'd be okay.

"You had your people who were skinny and you had the other extreme, and I was one of the people on the other extreme. It wasn't the norm. Yet my parents gave me all the confidence in the world that no matter how it looked, or no matter what, they expected a lot from me.

"My mother left the character trait in me always to be humble and meek, but also to be strong. As I was growing up, my dad was pretty much a disciplinarian, but I think one of the biggest traits he left was always to be prayerful."

MY ROLE MODEL
KEN RUETTGERS

When things got tough for my father, he refused to take the easy way out. For that alone I would love and honor Dad. But there's so much more he did for my siblings and me. That's why my number one role model in life is Ron Ruettgers, my dad.

Every day of my life I recognize his influence and realize what a remarkable difference he made in my life.

When I was very young, my mother died, leaving my father with three young boys. I was eight; my brother Steve was six; and Paul was just a baby. He was a year old.

Many relatives and friends tried to convince my dad that it might be better for everyone if he would split us up among other families who could better care for us. Although the offers were generous and well-intentioned, Dad held strong to what he knew was in our family's best interest—staying together.

He knew it wasn't going to be easy, but he had staying power. There was a way out if he wanted to take it. But he held strong in his beliefs and received strength through his faith in God.

During the day, Dad worked as a civil engineer. Then he would come home and start his other job: cooking, cleaning, and caring for his boys—day after day after day. I don't think he could have done it without the help of close friends and relatives who would bring over meals, watch us after school, and occasionally let us sleep over at their house.

Because I have three children of my own, I often think about the enormous sacrifice, commitment to responsibility, and determination that our father modeled for us and for others within his circle of influence.

Occasionally, friends of my father's will introduce themselves to me and tell me how grateful they are for the example he provided in their lives.

As with all good role models, his influence went far beyond his children. His actions spoke volumes to those who stood on the sidelines of his life and observed him in action.

My dad never knew he was influencing other people's lives, but it's obvious to us now that he was. He didn't do it through the platforms of professional athletics, enormous wealth, or awe-inspiring power. He lived a normal lifestyle, but with grace and faith.

I sometimes feel that if I can leave a legacy of virtues and character traits in my children like he left in his children, then I will consider myself successful. Even today, there is nothing more important to my Dad than his family.

He attended almost all of the events of our lives as we grew up. It didn't matter if it were a football game or a piano recital. He encouraged areas that interested his children, and he immersed himself in those areas. That's what he is leaving in the lives of his children. I see those traits in myself and my brothers and sister.

Two years after Mom died, Dad married a woman who assisted him in shaping and influencing our lives. Today, both of them still take an active roll in positively influencing other lives.

No wonder I'm interested in role models. I had the best, and all I can do is hope to be half the example he was for me and so many others.

PERSONAL TIME-OUT

1. Who's been the most influential person in my life? Think of several magical moments with that person that especially impacted you.

2. Who are 5 people I think I'm making an impact on with my life? What do I think each of them is learning from me—both good and bad?

3. Which of these legacy profiles most touched me? What did they teach me about the value of a good role model?

4. As I look at my children, what kind of legacy do I want to leave them? What one thing do I would hope my children will remember about me in 25 years?

RUETTGER'S REFLECTIONS

Football truths that also work in real life

All you can ask an individual to give is everything he has.

It's the total package that counts.

If you haven't made someone else's highlight film, it's because you're sitting on the bench.

NOTES

CHAPTER 1

1. Karl Malone, "One Role Model to Another," *Sports Illustrated*, (December 13, 1993).

2. *USA Today*, 1 July 1994.

3. Ric Telander, "The Wrong People for the Job," *Sports Illustrated* (December 23, 1991).

4. Paul Attner, "A Culture of Irresponsibility," *Sporting News*, (March 28, 1994).

5. Paul Attner, "The Hero Worshipper," *Sporting News* (March 28, 1994).

CHAPTER 2

1. James Dobson, *Focus on the Family*, (June 1994).

2. George W. Cornell, "Media Tune Out to Religion."

3. "We've Got Your Number," *New Man* (January-February 1994).

4. *Rolling Stone* (September 16, 1993).

5. *Los Angeles Times*, 5 August 1994.

6. Michael Medved, *Hollywood versus America* (New York: Harkper Collins, 1992), 147.

7. "Christians Also Want Their MTV," *New Man* (January-February 1995).

8. Rush Limbaugh, *See, I Told You So* (New York: Pocket Books), 196.

9. Steve Farrar, *Standing Tall* (Sisters, Ore.: Multnomah Books, 1994).

CHAPTER 3

1. "Whom Do America's Teens Respect?" *Parade* (November 29, 1994), 14.

2. "The Daddyless Society," *Futurist* (November-December 1992).

3. "The Changing American Family."

4. Nancy R. Gibbs, "Bringing Up Father," *Time* (june 28, 1993).

5. Linda Chavez, "Quayle Was Right on Family Values," *USA Today*, September 1994.

6. Edward Gilbreath, "The Great Awakening," *Christianity Today* (February 6, 1995).

7. Joseph P. Shapiro and Joannie M.Schrof, "Honor Thy Children," *U.S. News and World Report* (February 27, 1995).

8. David Blankenhorn, "Life Without Father," *USA Weekend*, 24-26 February 1995.

9. Edward Gilbreath, "Do We Really Need Fathers?" *Christianity Today* (February 6, 1995).

10. Blankenhorn, "Life Without Father."

11. *The South Bend Tribune*, 3 July 1994, Sunday Scene.

12. Scott Minerbrook, "Lives Without Father," *U.S. News and World Report* (February 27, 1995).

CHAPTER 4

1. *Focus on the Family Bulletin*, (1989), and quoted in *Josh McDowell Research Statistical Digest*, 87.

2. "Hell's Bells," in *Dangers of Rock and Roll*, part 1 of The Power of Music, quoting from American Academy of Pediatrics.

CHAPTER 5

1. Robert Hicks, *The Masculine Journey* (Colorado Springs: NavPress), 179.

2. Howard Hendricks, *New Man* (July/August 1994).

3. Paul Attner, "A Culture of Irresponsibility," Sporting News (March 28, 1994).

4. Ibid.

5. "Responsible Reggie White: Thanks on Hope," *USA Today*, 2 March 1995.

CHAPTER 6

1. Words and Music by Wayne Watson, "Somewhere In The World," © 1985 by Word Music (a div. of Word, Inc.) All rights reserved. Used by permission.

2. Josh and Dotty McDowell, *New Man* (November-December 1994).

CHAPTER 7

1. Tommy Evans, *New Man* (July-August 1994).

2. Edward Gilbreath, "The Great Awakening," *Christianity Today* (February 6, 1995).

CHAPTER 8

1. John Wooden, *They Call Me Coach* (Waco, Tex.: Word Publishing).

2. "What is a Hero," attrib. Jimmy Steward, quoted by Doris Lee McCoy, *Megatraits: Twelve traits of successful people* (Plano, Tex.: Wordward Publishing, Inc., 1988).

3. Peggy Ellsberg, "What's Wrong With Family Values," *America* (April 3, 1993).

4. Paul D. Kroger, "Integrity at Work," *New Man* (November-December 1994).

5. "Fresh Voices," *Parade*, (May 1, 1994).

CHAPTER 9

1. Bill Hybels, "Your Wife, Fit to be Treasured," *New Man* (January-February 1995).

2. Gary Smalley, "Promise Keepers," *New Man* (July-August 1994).

3. Howard Hendricks, *New Man* (July-August 1994).

CHAPTER 10

1. Joy Becker and Dan Dean, "I Want To Be Just Like You," (St. Louis: Praisesong Press).

CHAPTER 12

1. "Memories of Dad," *New Man* (May-June 1995).

2. Ibid.